Happy Birthday
To Arline
from
(1988) Mom.
Father Williams
conducted Holy Eucharist
today at 12 noon
Arline administered
the ~~chalice~~ - first time.
chalice

# BLIZZARD!

## The Great Storm of '88

# *Washington City, Sunday, March 11, 1888—7 A. M.*

**Indications for 24 hours, commencing at 3 P. M., Sunday, March 11, 1888.**

Fresh to brisk easterly winds, with rain, will prevail to-night, followed on Monday by colder brisk westerly winds and fair weather throughout the Atlantic states; colder fresh westerly winds, with fair weather, over the lake regions, the Ohio and Mississippi valleys; diminishing northerly winds, with slightly colder, fair weather, in the Gulf states; light to fresh variable winds, with higher temperature, in Kansas, Nebraska, and Colorado.

**SIGNALS.—Cautionary** southeast signals are displayed on the Atlantic coast from Norfolk section to Wood's Holl section.

**RIVERS.—The rivers will rise slightly.**

*The War Department Signal Service under the direction of A. W. Greely was responsible for this official daily weather forecast.*

# BLIZZARD!

## The Great Storm of '88

by Judd Caplovich

Edited by Wayne W. Westbrook, Ph.D.

VeRo Publishing Company
1987

This book is dedicated to Historical Societies, Libraries and Museums—Without their assistance and collections this book would not be possible— To them goes my heartfelt appreciation—Please use them and support them.

# Table of Contents

# List of Photographs, Illustrations and Newspapers

# Acknowledgements

I wish to thank the following libraries, historical societies, museums and individuals for their help in making materials in their collections available for this book.

Albany Institute of History and Art, Albany, NY
American Antiquarian Society, Worcester, MA
American Meteorological Society, Boston, MA
The Antiquarian and Landmarks Society, Hartford, CT
Barnes Museum, Southington, CT
Bergenfield Museum Society, Bergenfield, NJ
Berkshire County Historical Society, Pittsfield, MA
George S. Bolster, Saratoga Springs, NY
Brattleboro P.H.O.T.O.S., Brattleboro, VT
Bridgeport Public Library, Bridgeport, CT
Bristol Historical Society, Bristol, CT
Brooklyn Historical Society, Brooklyn, NY
Brown University Library, Providence, RI
Central Connecticut State University Library, New Britain, CT
Mary Cheney Library, Manchester, CT
Cheshire County Historical Society, Keene, NH
Wayne R. Cogan, West Hartford, CT
The Connecticut Historical Society, Hartford, CT
Connecticut National Bank, North Manchester, CT
Connecticut State Library, Hartford, CT
Darien Historical Society, Darien, CT
Delaware State Archives, Dover, DE
Derby Public Library, Derby, CT
Dutchess County Historical Society, Poughkeepsie, NY
East Hartford Public Library, East Hartford, CT
Fairfield County Historical Society, Fairfield, CT
Falls Village Historical Society, Falls Village, CT
Fitchburg Historical Society, Fitchburg, MA
Historical Society of Greenfield, Greenfield, MA
Hartford Public Library, Hartford, CT
Hempstead Public Library, Hempstead, NY
Huntington Historical Society, Huntington, NY
Keene Public Library, Keene, NH
Paul J. Kocin, NASA/Goddard Space Flight Center, Greenbelt, MD
The Library of Congress, Washington, DC
David Ludlum, Princeton, NJ
Manchester Historic Association, Manchester, NH
Manchester Public Library, Manchester, NH
Meriden Historical Society, Meriden, CT
Middlesex County Historical Society, Middletown, CT

Museum of the City of New York, New York, NY
The National Archives, Washington, DC
The National Museum of American History, Washington, DC
Jack Naylor Private Museum, Boston, MA
New Canaan Historical Society, New Canaan, CT
New Hampshire State Library, Concord, NH
New Haven Colony Historical Society, New Haven, CT
The New Jersey Historical Society, Newark, NJ
The New York Historical Society, New York, NY
New York Public Library, New York, NY
New York State Library, Albany, NY
Daniel Nichols, Manchester, CT
Northampton Historical Society, Northampton, MA
Northport Historical Society, Northport, NY
Old Derby Historical Society, Ansonia, CT
Dr. Marvin A. Oleshansky, Silver Spring, MD
Orange Historical Society, Orange, MA
Ossining Historical Society, Ossining, NY
Historical Society of Pennsylvania, Philadelphia, PA
Pennsylvania State Library, Harrisburg, PA
Plainville Historical Society, Plainville, CT
Queens Library, Jamaica, NY
Rensselaer County Historical Society, Troy, NY
Rockingham Public Library, Bellows Falls, VT
Roselle Park Historical Society, Roselle Park, NJ
Historical Society of Saratoga Springs, Saratoga Springs, NY
Springfield Public Library, Springfield, MA
Torrington Historical Society, Torrington, CT
Trinity College Library, Hartford, CT
Trumbull Historical Society, Trumbull, CT
Mark Twain Memorial, Hartford, CT
University of Connecticut Library, Storrs, CT
Vermont State Library, Montpelier, VT
Vernon Historical Society, Vernon, CT
West Hartford Public Library, West Hartford, CT
West Springfield Historical Society, West Springfield, MA
Westboro Historical Society, Westboro, MA
Wilton Historical Society, Wilton, CT
Worcester Public Library, Worcester, MA
Yale, Sterling Library, New Haven, CT

# Foreword

I've endeavored to put together a comprehensive photographic and meteorological journal on the Northeast's severest and most renowned snowstorm. This storm has been referred to as the Great Storm of 1888, the Blizzard from Michigan, the Big Snow of 1888 and the Town Meeting Day Blizzard, but it will always be remembered as the Blizzard of 1888 or just the Blizzard of '88. The book contains more than 300 photographs showing how widespread the deep snow was and many illustrations from such popular national news magazines as *Harper's Weekly, Frank Leslie's* and *The Scientific American,* which showed the rest of the nation how severe the storm was, in factual, exaggerated and often humorous detail. Included here also are detailed weather maps, a snowfall table with almost 500 reported measurements at the time and a snowfall map with some recent corrections. These measurements and the accompanying snowfall chart prepared from them are only estimates, as the heavy drifting made it difficult to record the snowfall accurately.

The storm paralyzed and isolated every city and town from Washington, DC, north through New England and west through central Pennsylvania and New York for up to a week. Nearly all commerce and industry, including Wall Street, came to a halt because thousands of telegraph, telephone and electrical wires were severed, hundreds of ships were damaged, with over 200 boats sunk from Georgia to New England, and trains—the most important form of transportation—as well as other forms of public transportation, were completely blockaded. Food and fuel quickly became in short supply, which added to the hardships that northeasterners had to bear.

Except for the trains—and even they weren't up to the task—the only way to clear off the snow was by manual labor, horses and oxen. The one blessing about this storm was that it came late in the season. The temperature didn't stay below freezing very long, and the snow melted rather quickly, without causing widespread serious flooding. In all, it could have been a much worse disaster and hardship.

Even though the first "Blizzard of '88" occurred January 12–14 in the west—from the Dakotas south to Texas and Montana east to Wisconsin—plunging temperatures to as low as −52°F, killing 237 people (a vast number for such a sparsely populated area) and wasting tens of thousands of head of cattle and other livestock, the great storm in the Northeast of March 11–14 is the one most remembered. This storm dumped 30 to 50 inches of snow over a widespread area of the Northeast with winds of 40 to 70 mph on land and up to 90 mph at sea. It took an estimated 400 lives and caused an estimated $20 million in property losses, a sum equal to hundreds of millions of dollars today.

Other than the Civil War, which was commissioned to be documented by professional photographers, this journal records one of the earliest large-scale disasters in actual photographs, by both amateurs and professionals. Many blizzard images, however, have suffered from fading after a hundred years' effects of dampness and ultraviolet light. The better quality photographs are used here, and, where necessary, some weaker ones that show important scenes are included.

The historical narrative was derived from the many contemporary newspaper accounts and weather summaries of the time, diaries and other published personal accounts. Also referenced are some of the few books, pamphlets and articles published since the blizzard, Dave Ludlum's many weather books and Paul Kocin's research and report in the November 1983 *Bulletin of the American Meteorological Society.*

This work is the most accurate, detailed and illustrated history of the Blizzard of '88 published to date. It will help preserve these photos and will undoubtedly prove to be the standard reference source and "Official Guide" to the *BLIZZARD! The Great Storm of '88.*

Judd Caplovich

**LOST AT SEA.**

Fearful Storm on the Delaware.

Vessels Wrecked and Crews Lost.

Shipping Damaged $500,000.

Only Five of N Recove...

Prisoners on Ice Twenty-Four Hours.

**WIRES ARE DOWN.**

Washington Cut Off by a Storm of Great Severity.

NEW YORK, March 11.—This evening, shortly after 7 o'clock, telegraphic communication with Washington was suddenly interrupted, and up to this hour (9.30) the wires to that city have not been restored. The Western Union and Postal Telegraph companies are unable to reach any one south of Baltimore. Chicago, with which city communication is bad by way of Buffalo, reports that nothing can be heard from Washington. Baltimore reports that a heavy storm has prevailed all day in that locality, and it is evident that its fury has to-night assumed the proportions of a hurricane in the immediate neighborhood of Washington.

*The Blizzard of 1888 turned North Pearl Street in Albany, New York, into an avant garde sculpture garden with Mother Nature as both the artist and gallery owner. These untouched drifts offer mute testimony to the storm's snow-slinging capabilities. (Albany Institute of History and Art)*

# Chapter 1 — The Storm Begins

From Washington, D.C., to New England on March 11, 1888, a steady and chilling rain fell on churchgoers returning home to Sunday dinner. Most who huddled under umbrellas or braved a drenching as they walked on cobblestone streets and country lanes viewed the weather as a reminder that winter still held a failing grip on the northeastern corner of the United States. The blustery afternoon seemed like the last gasp of a season that had already made its mark as being the mildest winter in 17 years.

Spring gave signs of early arrival. Trees budded. Purple and yellow crocuses debuted. The vernal equinox — the day when meteorologists and astronomers mark the official beginning of spring — was barely a week and a half away. Already farmers were cultivating and preparing their fields; many expected to put seed into the ground by next week. Even Walt Whitman, then employed as the staff poet of the *New York Herald*, was taken by the spirit of the season, penning a short work to appear in Monday's edition titled ''The First Dandelion'':

> Simple and fresh and fair from winter's close emerging.
> As if no artifice of fashion, business, politics had ever been.
> Forth from its sunny nook of shelter'd grace — innocent, golden, calm
> as the dawn,
> The spring's first dandelion shows its trustful face.

*Heavy ropes keep a derailed locomotive in Naugatuck, Connecticut, from toppling over as workmen attempt to clear the tracks around it. (Fairfield County Historical Society)*

What more could the Sunday afternoon downpour be than a harbinger of the warmer showers of spring to soon transform the dusty brown of late winter into verdure and flowers.

When the precipitation stopped 72 hours later, an estimated 400 persons, including 200 in New York City alone, would be dead or dying, property damage would total an estimated $20,000,000 and stricken cities along the east coast of the United States would face the enormous problem of what to do with tons upon tons of snow, the largest amount to fall in two and a half centuries of habitation.

No one expected the Great Blizzard of 1888. To most East Coast residents accustomed to milder winter snowstorms, its arrival was a surprise party of the worst kind.

The *New York Times*, ordinarily the staid chronicler of events of the day, vividly described the Blizzard's fury.

> The wind had the power of slinging snow into doorways and packing it up against the doors, and sifting it through window panes, of piling it up in high drifts at street corners and twirling it into hard mounds . . . such as New Yorkers had never seen before. For the first times in their lives, they knew what a western blizzard was.
> The wind's spite was shown in driving showers of sleet and ice shot into one's face that stung worse than the stings of modest hornets.

Vermonters, accustomed to hard winters, were more succinct. With a style that favorite son Calvin Coolidge would make famous when he became President 45 years later, the *Bellows Falls Times* laconically described the scene:

> No paths, no streets, no sidewalks, no light, no roads, no guests, no calls, no teams, no hacks, no trains, no moon, no meat, no milk, no paper, no mails, no news, no thing — but snow.

The Army's Signal Service, precursor of the United States Weather Bureau that would come under the Department of Agriculture's civilian control three years later, predicted "light to fresh easterly winds with warmer, fair weather" for New York, New Jersey and Pennsylvania in a report published in the March 10 *New York Times*. The *Times* reported similar weather for New England with winds blowing from the north to be followed by a drop in temperature.

*Top left: The fierce winds blew over tall telegraph poles on Manhattan's Tenth Avenue as if they were tomato stakes, poking out upper story windows in the process. (Museum of the City of New York)*

*Top right: A young boy leans against a massive snow drift blocking the sidewalk on New York's Madison Ave. near 50th Street. (The New York Historical Society)*

*The snow roller was a common sight on New England streets after snowstorms in the late 19th century. Its purpose was to pack down rather than clear the snow, helping the passage of vehicles on runners. (Brattleboro P.H. O.T.O.S.)*

*Brokers and financiers survey the damage done by the Blizzard to the telegraph and telephone links connecting Wall Street with the outside world. This photograph was taken on New Street looking toward Wall Street. (The New York Historical Society)*

## Thoughts of the Times

Thoughts other than snow occupied the minds of persons coming home from church on that rainy Sunday afternoon. Across the Atlantic, Kaiser Wilhelm I of Germany had just died at age 90. Flags flew at half mast as German-Americans mourned the loss and wondered what direction the country would take as his son, Frederick III of Prussia, assumed the throne. The new ruler's health and ability to govern were already called into question. Rumors flowed that he suffered from throat cancer and was not expected to live much longer. Student disturbances in Russia protested the spying system of supervision and called for reform of educational statutes. The disorders were quelled swiftly by the czar's troops.

At home, the previous week ended mixed on Wall Street as buyers and sellers assessed the scandal resulting from a stock trading scheme by Richmond Terminal Company directors. The impact of a strike against the Chicago, Burlington & Quincy railroad sent several transportation stocks to new yearly lows. Stationers announced they would band together to fight the issuance of stamped envelopes by the post office, a move they saw as undue government interference in private business.

Incumbent President Grover Cleveland began his campaign for a second term and expected renomination as the Democratic candidate. Republicans tended to favor the scandal-tainted James Blaine, but Benjamin Harrison's name was heard as a dark-horse candidate.

For the well-to-do, entertainment was in abundance. New York boasted four premieres of new dramatic works, plus a performance of a stage version of *La Tosca* at the Broadway Theatre. In more conservative cities like Hartford, theatre devotees were decrying the "things in the play [La Tosca] which must shock sensitive natures and religious ones." Shakespeare's comedy *A Midsummer Night's Dream* was playing at Daly's Theatre for those seeking a more classical theatrical experience.

Those less prosperous had to be content with circus extravaganzas like P.T. Barnum's new exposition in New York's Madison Square Garden, where a fifty-cent general admission ticket allowed the holder to view "the finest assembly of trained animals since Noah." Performances were scheduled to begin Monday, March 12 at 2 p.m.

As society pages gossiped about the lifestyles of the rich and famous, listing those who would be neighbors of the Astors and Vanderbilts this season in Newport's "cottages" by the sea, Irish-Americans announced plans for a grand St. Patrick's Day parade to be held the following Saturday. New York Mayor Abram S. Hewitt respectfully declined an invitation to review the marchers.

Shoppers anticipated the new spring fashions, and many patrons planned to queue up outside retailers' doors when they opened on Monday. That weekend large New York department stores advertised the latest clothing styles for both men and women.

Only a four-line item buried at the bottom of page 13 in the March 9 *New York Times* gave a preview of the disaster that was about to befall the largest population centers in North America. A blizzard raged in northern Minnesota. From Duluth a dispatch reported that no trains had arrived from anywhere south of that Lake Superior city on Friday.

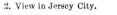

# THE SWATH OF THE STORM

**Terrible Effects of Wind and Snow in the Country.**

---

**WIRES DOWN AND RAILROADS BLOCKED**

---

**Passengers Keeping Warm with Difficulty and Stock Freezing.**

---

**SUFFERINGS OF TRAIN HANDS.**

---

**Streets Impassble from the Drifts and Farmhouses Buried**

---

**SOME BRIGHT LIGHTS ON A DARK PICTURE.**

---

**Wreck of Vessels and Loss of Life on the Coast.**

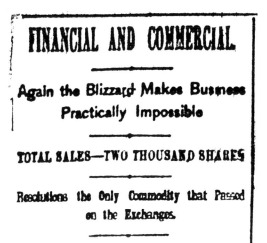

2. View in Jersey City.

# FINANCIAL AND COMMERCIAL

---

**Again the Blizzard Makes Business Practically Impossible**

---

**TOTAL SALES—TWO THOUSAND SHARES**

---

**Resolutions the Only Commodity that Passed on the Exchanges.**

*The show must go on. A placard advertises a matinee performance at Albany's Leland Opera House on the day after the Blizzard. (Albany Institute of History and Art)*

5

# STAMFORD DESTROYED.

## Terrrrible Disaster to a Thriving Connecticut Town.

## FIRE AT CLIFTON SPRINGS

### The Clifton House Block Burned, and Two Men Injured.

## THE GREAT EASTERN BLIZZARD.

### Not of Wide Extent, but of Concentrated Energy.

#### STAMFORD BURNED.

[Special Despatch to The Albany Times.]

SPRINGFIELD, Mass., March 13.—The village of Stamford, Conn., as reported by a special despatch, was totally destroyed by fire early this morning. Wires are down and particulars are not obtainable.  L. B.

*Residents of Manhattan's West 18th Street clear a sidewalk-blocking drift that reached to the top of gas street lamps. (Connecticut State Library)*

A DRIFT IN W. 18 ST.

# THE BURIED CITY

## New York's Dreadful Sepulture Under Masses of Snow.

## A NIGHT OF DEVASTATION.

### How the Tempest Howled and Raged Through the Dark Wilderness of Streets.

## PERISHING MEN AND WOMEN

### Wanderers Found Dead in Snowdrifts and Families Driven Into the Storm by Fire.

## AND THE TEMPERATURE BELOW ZERO.

### Coal Going Up, Supplies Giving Out and Communications of All Kinds Jarred.

## PARTIAL RESUMPTION OF TRAVEL.

### The Elevated Roads and Ferries Running but No Attempt to Move the Horse Cars.

### SNOWED UP TRAINS IN THE COUNTRY

### The Storm Abating Yesterday but Its Effects Disastrous.

## COLEMAN'S STUPENDOUS TASK

### Twenty-three Million Loads of Snow Below Forty-second Street.

# SILENCE.

## The Wires All Down.

### Many Railway Trains Stalled.

### Snowed Under on N. E. Roads.

### Ice Packed Solidly on the Tracks.

### The Western Union Co. in a Bad Fix.

### News by Long-Distance Telephone Only.

### Workingmen Housed in a Car All Night,

### Storm-Swept Revere Beach ---Great Desolation.

### Cottages Destroyed and Bulkheads Wrecked.

### Two Holyoke Factories Crushed in by the Weight of Snow.

### South Shore Seas Sweeping Over Minot's.

## A 500-Year Event

Despite having occurred a century ago, the Blizzard of '88 is still the benchmark by which other violent and severe winter storms are measured. From March 11 to March 14, 1888, this intensely powerful storm battered the northeastern United States with an unprecedented combination of heavy snows, high winds and bitterly cold temperatures. Twenty- to fifty-inch snow depths were recorded across sections of New England, New York, New Jersey and Pennsylvania, accompanied by winds blowing up to 80 miles per hour and temperatures that dropped close to 0°F.

The Great Blizzard of 1888 has no peer in sheer force and destructiveness. More bitter cold waves and heavier snowfalls have struck the northeast in the century since the Blizzard, but never with such a ravaging one-two punch. No meteorological event in the region matches the overwhelming and paralyzing devastation caused by this snowstorm. Records kept by weather watchers in the century before the storm and those on file since then fail to note any storm in the northeast that can match the intensity of the 1888 Blizzard. Meteorologists describe the Blizzard as a 500-year event — a storm of such ferocity that it could only be expected to occur once in half a millennium.

In addition to the meteorological records set by the storm, the Blizzard of '88 made an indelible mark in the memory of the population living at the time of the storm. Never before had the political and economic centers of the nation been so paralyzed. Never had the transportation and distribution system been shut down as completely as it was during the Blizzard. Citizens accustomed to rapid delivery of information through telegraphed

*This wreck on the New York and Harlem Railroad occurred when several locomotives tried to crash through a massive drift near Coleman's Station, New York. Four railroad workers were killed. (The New York Historical Society)*

*Furs, a knit cap, and a long double-breasted coat kept Mrs. Emma Farnsworth warm as she braved the snow-covered sidewalks of Albany, New York. (Albany Institute of History and Art)*

*A young Vermonter contemplates the drifts ten to fifteen feet high that choked the streets of Bellows Falls, Vermont. (Rockingham Public Library)*

reports to local newspapers suddenly found themselves cut off in total darkness. For those mid-March days, towns and cities in the northeast might just as well have been set back in medieval Europe. The Blizzard rendered 19th century industrial progress useless for a time and made it, for all who survived, an unforgettable experience.

Newspapers of the day boasted about the storm in their front page stories. "Now We Know What A Dakota Blizzard Is" clarioned the headline in one New York daily. It was a matter of pride echoed by almost everyone. All knew what it was like to be a survivor. All had a story to tell. The Blizzard Men of 1888, a group of gaffers who met once a year from 1929 until the early 1970s, related tales about snowdrifts that got deeper with each telling. Decades later, grandchildren and great-grandchildren of those who had seen the Blizzard heard stories about how the whirling mists of snow dazzled and confused the eye or about how dreadfully cold it was.

Would a similar-sized blizzard today generate such excitement or drama? Probably not as much. Satellites perched in geosynchronous orbits 22,000 miles above the equator could spot a developing storm center early, taking away the element of surprise. Weather forecasters using supercomputers would then figure out in a hurry what would happen when a cold front smacked into a warm front. Alerted by news bulletins, anyone worried about not getting to the store after it was over would fill up the freezer ahead of time. The public today would not be taken by surprise as they were a hundred years ago.

# Chapter 2 — Anatomy of the Blizzard

The Great Blizzard of 1888 raised professional interest among meteorologists, besides stimulating the public's curiosity. Three characteristics made it a phenomenon among storms of the era. First, the storm developed with unprecedented rapidity. Second, the excessive amounts of precipitation set records that still have not been broken a century later. Last, the combination of wind, snow and sheer force of the Blizzard caused damage and casualties far beyond anything such a wide geographical area of the United States had ever experienced.

A meteorological analysis of the Blizzard of '88 is somewhat impeded by the limited data that weather observers of the day were able to gather. Animated satellite photographs allowing minute-by-minute forecasts of the route of destruction were, of course, unavailable. Even weather balloons, the meteorologist's standard tool in the days before radar, were not available to analyze the extent of upper atmosphere disturbances, and wouldn't be until 60 years after the storm. Transmission and exchange of charts and weather maps were possible only by mail — facsimile machines and computer graphics being far off in the future. No information from points anywhere on the Atlantic Ocean was available either, at least not in time to be useful. Instrument readings from vessels at sea were recorded only in ships' logs — valuable knowledge perhaps for the meteorological historian, but impractical to the forecaster who wanted to meet deadlines for the next morning's newspaper.

In 1888, The United States Signal Service operated a telegraphic network of 170 surface observers who filed reports three times a day at 7 a.m., 3 p.m. and 10 p.m. from most major cities. Measurements included uncorrected readings of barometric pressure, dry and wet bulb temperature, dew point temperature, relative humidity, wind velocity and direction, cloudiness, precipitation, current weather, and totals and averages for a variety of meteorological quantities. Some 2,000 volunteer observers under the direction of the Smithsonian Institution and the Surgeon General's office augmented these reports. Detailed surface analysis of weather patterns over the land was possible using the information gathered by this network of observers. With the telegraphic data in hand, individual forecasters could discern regional and national weather trends.

*A pompous and rotund homeowner, whose girth exceeds the width of the path cleared on the sidewalk, confronts the hired laborer in this humorous engraving from* Harper's Weekly. *The caption reads: "See here, man, is that the best you can do for a path in front of my house?" "Scuze me, Boss, but the missus told me not ter be too p'tikeler — jes git a path made so's yer might git hum. She'd ought ter have given me yer size. Try it sideways." (Connecticut State Library)*

## Tracing the Storm's Progress

Most meteorologists agree that the Blizzard of 1888 was the result of two storms. The Signal Service had observed two areas of low pressure a day or so before the Blizzard; one over the Gulf of Mexico, the other over the Great Lakes. Both appeared to be strong storm centers. At the Pensacola, Florida, weather station the Signal Service observer reported 4.05 inches of rain fell on March 10. Further north, this rain would have produced 40 inches of snow.

Surface weather maps of March 9, 1888, disclose very little that was unusual in the weather patterns. Skies were mostly clear across the northeastern United States with afternoon temperatures ranging from 30° to 40°F, a typical weather pattern for late winter. A slowly moving cold front sort of bisected the nation from Minnesota to Texas. Temperature readings varied considerably on opposite sides of the front, with highs in the 70s over Texas and Oklahoma and lows in the teens in western Nebraska. Two low pressure centers were noted: one in Iowa, the other reaching from Colorado to the Texas panhandle.

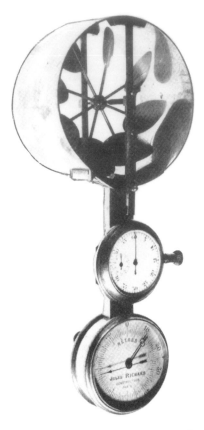

Windmill anemometer "Jules Richard Constructeur Paris" (The National Museum of American History)

Noted Arctic explorer Adolphus Greely headed the United States Signal Services, the agency charged with weather forecasting, at the time of the Blizzard. (The National Archives)

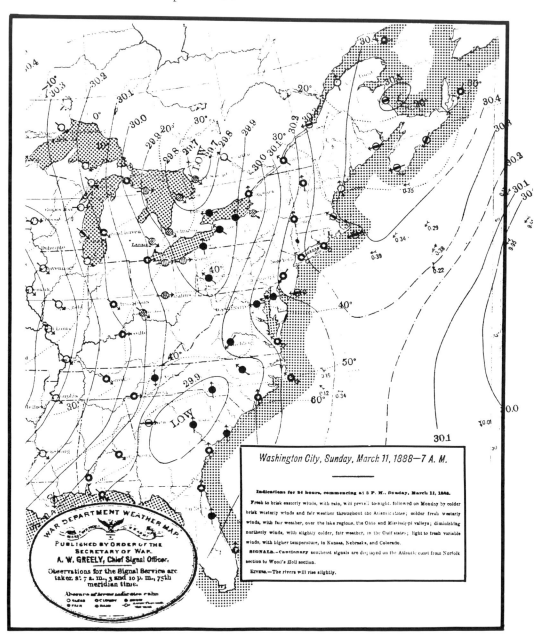

The Colorado low was probably the same one reported a few days earlier on the California coast, and was associated with heavy snow in Salt Lake City, Utah, the preceding day. As it moved southeast toward the Gulf of Mexico, it dropped drizzle and light rain, causing a few thunderstorms in eastern Texas. The movement of the storm center over the warm waters of the Gulf dragged moisture-laden air ahead of the cold front into the midwest. This produced showers throughout the region and light snow in the Great Lakes states. As the cold front moved east, observers reported deeper snows through Minnesota, Wisconsin and Michigan, while a dusting was seen in Appalachian Mountain areas of Kentucky and eastern Tennessee. Frost laced the ground as far south as Louisiana and Mississippi.

On Saturday night and early Sunday morning, the storm's movement began to swing to the northeast, bringing it across Florida's panhandle and Georgia where barometers fell to 29.88 inches of mercury. The dip in the Gulf of Mexico had revitalized and intensified the storm. On Sunday morning the storm that had slowly crossed the nation during the past week was transformed into a dangerous tempest with high winds and heavy precipitation.

Rain was now widespread along much of the east coast of the United States, with precipitation reported at points as far apart as Buffalo, Pittsburgh, Washington, D.C., and Roanoke, Virginia. A dark blanket of clouds spread into New England as a high pressure center moved off northeasterly into the Atlantic. By Sunday at 3 p.m., a trough anchored by two low pressure centers at each end extended in a curve bending toward the southeast from Ontario to Norfolk, Virginia. The counterclockwise rotation of winds around the trough moved a cold northwesterly gale out over the Atlantic Ocean, causing the storm to pick up additional moisture in the Gulf Stream. The storm consolidated further over open water, whipping the winds to nearly hurricane force. As the warm, saturated air met cooler temperatures over land, the moisture condensed to fall as rain and snow.

Ships ranging in size from small fishing schooners and pilot boats to the eight passenger liners that had sailed from New York on Saturday for destinations as varied as Halifax, New Orleans and Europe began to feel the storm's violence Sunday afternoon. Ships sailing south met the storm head on, while those bound for Europe and points north endured a lesser blow. At nightfall on Sunday the furious winds slammed into the coast, affecting the eastern seaboard from Cape Hatteras, North Carolina, to Montauk Point on Long Island.

At 5 p.m. Sunday the rain changed to snow as the front passed over Washington, D.C. Two hours later snow covered Baltimore's rain-slicked streets. By 10 p.m. three inches of snow whipped by 25-mile-per-hour winds swirled around the nation's capital, while Baltimore reported six inches.

More than an inch of rain had fallen on Philadelphia when the front passed through at 10 p.m. At the same time in New York City, where temperatures already hovered around the freezing point, streets and elevated railroad tracks, carts, streetcars, buildings, sidewalks, lampposts and everything out of doors developed a coating of ice from the wind-blown rain. Debris flew aimlessly about in the streets and ice-laden branches on trees snapped under the stress of weight and wind. Rain had spread into southwestern New England as well, and the easterly wind increased in intensity. Philadelphia's precipitation changed to snow at 11:15 p.m. New York's weather followed suit at midnight.

Cup anemometer "J.W. Queen & Co. Philadelphia" (The National Museum of American History)

Two thermometers forming a psychrometer, with a computing device, were patented by J. Winlock and J.S.F. Huddleston. (The National Museum of American History)

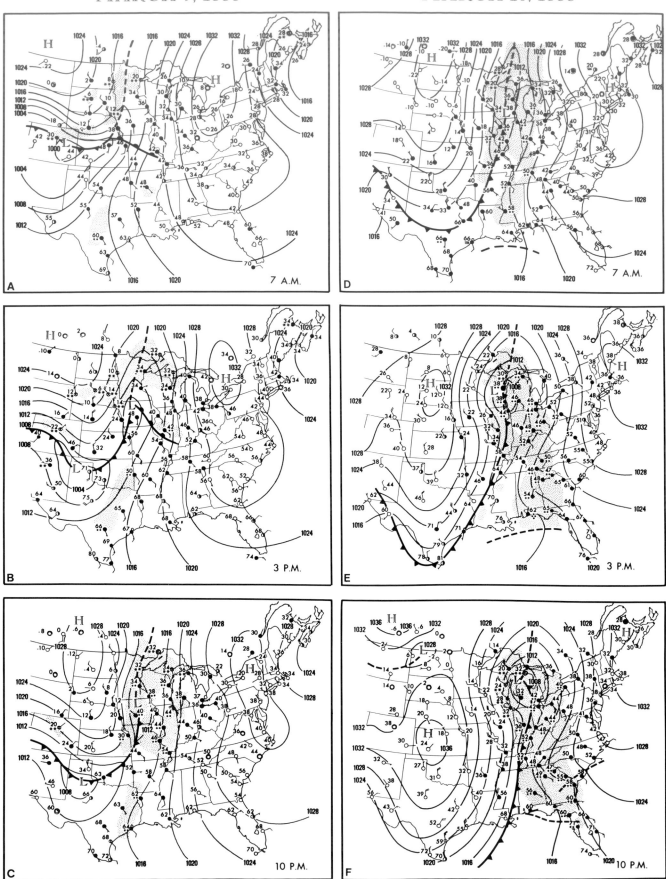

## MARCH 11, 1888

## MARCH 12, 1888

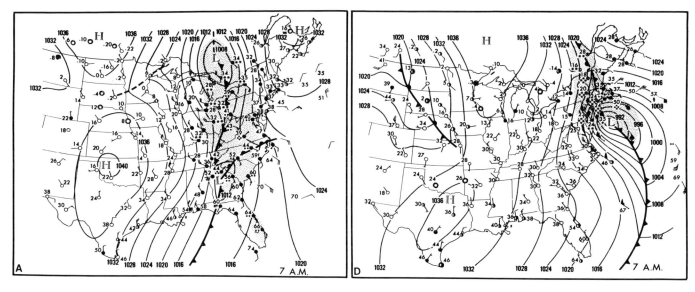

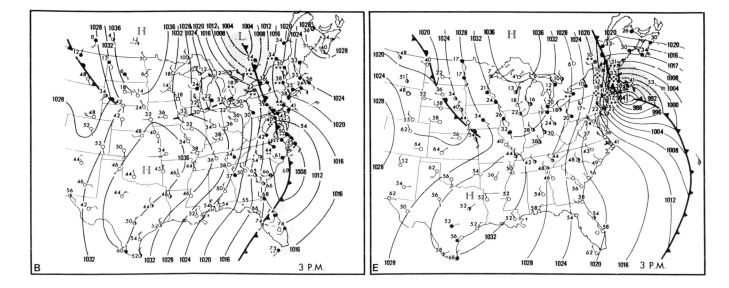

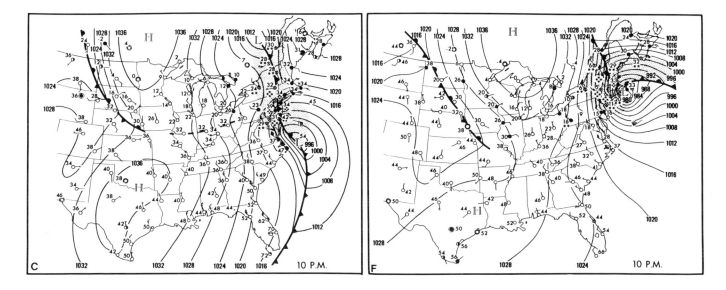

13

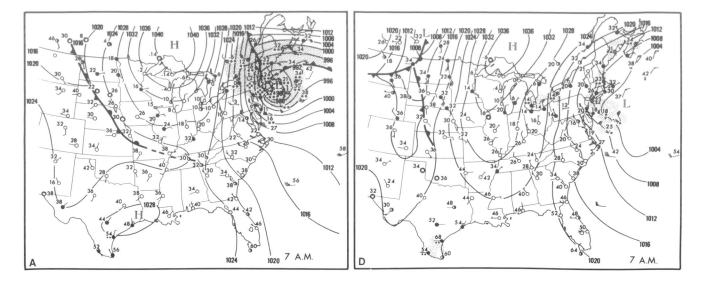

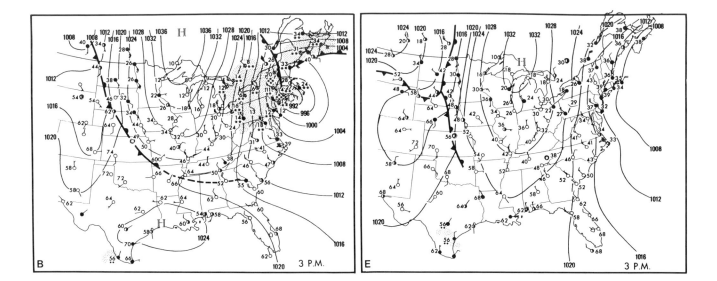

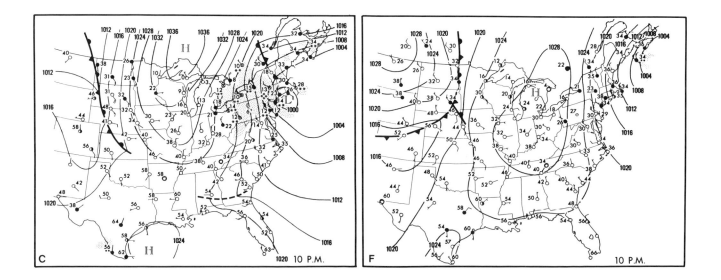

During the night, the storm continued to grow off shore. Several ships noted rapid drops in barometric pressure, a wind shift to the northwest with a tremendous increase in velocity, swiftly dropping temperatures and heavy snow. On board the New York pilot boat *Charles H. Marshall*, which had sailed Saturday afternoon from Staten Island on a routine voyage, the captain's log recorded the succession of changes in the weather:

*Thermograph "Richard Frères" (The National Museum of American History)*

> ... March 11. At 10 a.m., the pilots, who are good judges of the weather, thought by the threatening weather that there was going to be a storm, but not so bad a one as it proved to be. Put two more reefs in the sails and steered to the northward intending to go in for harbor if possible. At 4 p.m. it was blowing a moderate gale from SE, increasing at 5 p.m. to a strong gale . . . were then about 18 miles southeast from the lightship; but it shut down a dense fog, so would not run in, but concluded to stop out and take it as it came.

> March 12. At 2 a.m. wore around, the wind hauling to the east. At 3 a.m. the wind moderated, but the weather looked so threatening in the NW that the fourth reef was taken in the mainsail and treble reefed the foresail. At 3:30 a.m. the wind died out completely and the boat lay broadside on to the heavy SE sea, which was threatening to engulf the craft. At 3:55 a.m., it [the wind] came out from the NW with such force that the boat went over on her beam

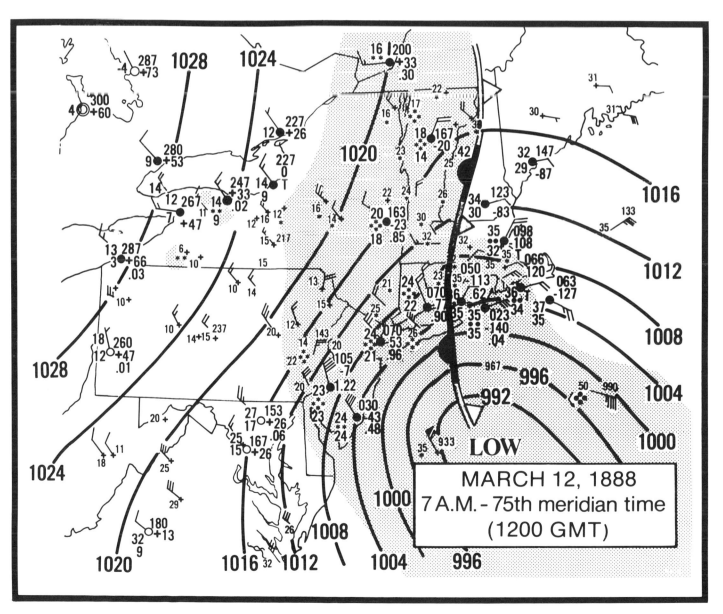

MARCH 12, 1888
7 A.M. – 75th meridian time
(1200 GMT)

*Electrical wind direction recorder "Richard Frères" (The National Museum of American History)*

*Daniel Draper's bimetallic thermograph (The National Museum of American History)*

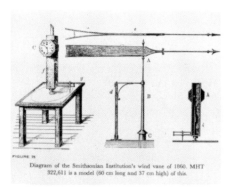

*Smithsonian Institution wind vane. (The National Museum of American History)*

ends, but righted up immediately. In two hours the boat was so much iced up by the snow and water that struck her that she resembled a small iceberg. At 8 a.m. the wind increased to a hurricane. Had to lower the foresail, but before the sail could be hauled down had to get iron bars and sledgehammers to beat the ice off the ropes and mast . . . seas by this time were running in every direction . . . The little vessel was in danger of being swamped. At 10 a.m. the snow and rain came with such force that it was impossible to look to windward.

Throughout Sunday night and the early hours of Monday morning, rain gradually spread over southwestern New England, but it quickly turned to heavy snow. New Haven recorded the beginning of a blinding snowfall at 2:30 a.m. By 7 a.m. Monday, snow had stopped falling across northern Virginia and Maryland, but the barrage was at its peak in New York and New England. The storm was centered in the ocean south of Long Island, and the front cut a north-south swath through the middle of New England separating cool maritime air to the east from increasingly colder air to the west. As the storm continued, a slow-moving high pressure system north of the Great Lakes induced even more colder air from Canada to funnel southward into New York, western New England, and the mid-Atlantic states. Another high, centered over the Gulf of St. Lawrence and Newfoundland, sandwiched the storm in position. These two highs probably were the elements responsible for the heavy snowfall because they helped stall the movement of the low pressure center for 48 hours.

By nightfall on Monday, the center of the storm had barely moved and was located near Block Island. Barometers touched bottom, registering the lowest points in years with 28.92 inches of mercury at Woods Hole, Massachusetts, and 28.98 in Providence, Rhode Island. Winds gusting up to 80 miles per hour swept an area from Nova Scotia south to Virginia. The icy blasts were felt more than 600 miles off shore at Bermuda. Heavy snows and blizzard conditions were the rule over much of the northeast. Temperatures west of the front had dipped to the single digits in many places. The temperature difference on opposite sides of the front was dramatic. When Northfield, Vermont, recorded 4°F on Monday night, Nashua, New Hampshire, 60 miles to the east basked in a comparatively balmy 34°F.

Blizzard conditions persisted through Tuesday morning from New Jersey northward as the storm remained locked in about the same position. Bitter cold enveloped the region with New York City recording a low of 5°F, a record for the date that still stands. Temperatures hovered near 0°F across much of New York and Pennsylvania. Signs suggested that the storm was getting weaker. Areas of snowfall had become less organized; some stations received heavy amounts while others nearby received lesser accumulation. The distinct boundary between areas of high and low temperature began to decay. As the storm passed over Block Island Sound toward Cape Cod, it faded almost as quickly as it had intensified during the weekend. Snow diminished during the day, but the storm still packed enough punch in places to deposit 10 or more inches of new accumulation on top of what had fallen on Monday.

Not until Wednesday morning did the storm center show some appreciable movement from its stationary position off Cape Cod. Reports from mariners pinpointed the Blizzard's remains about 200 miles southeast of Nova Scotia. The storm still had enough tenacity to cause unsettled conditions over an immense area of the Western Atlantic from Labrador to the Caribbean, and an additional inch or two of snow fell in many places across New York and New England. Finally relieved by a high pressure center

# NEW YORK METEOROLOGICAL OBSERVATORY
## CENTRAL PARK  MARCH, 1888  NEW YORK CITY

| | HYGROMETER | | | CLOUDS | | | RAIN AND SNOW | | | | | REMARKS | |
|---|---|---|---|---|---|---|---|---|---|---|---|---|---|
| DAY | RELATIVE HUMIDITY | | | CLEAR = 0 OVERCAST = 10 | | | DEPTH IN INCHES | | | | | | |
| | 7 AM | 2 PM | 9 PM | 7 AM | 2 PM | 9 PM | BEGINNING | ENDING | DURA-TION | WATER | SNOW | 7 AM | 2 PM |
| 10 | 75 | 90 | 88 | 0 | SE 4 CU | 7 CU | | | | | | MILD, PLEASANT | MILD, PLEASANT |
| 11 | 91 | 90 | 93 | 10 | 10 | 10 | 2:30 PM | 12:00 PM | 9:30 | .65 | | RAW, OVERCAST | COOL, OVERCAST |
| 12 | 100 | 100 | 100 | 10 | 10 | 10 | 0:00 AM | 5:30 PM | 17:30 | 1.45 | 21" | COLD, WINDY, SNOWING | COLD, WINDY SNOWING; SEVERE STORM |
| 13 | 100 | 100 | 100 | 10 | 10 | 10 | | | | | | COLD, WINDY | COLD, WINDY |
| 14 | 89 | 89 | 93 | 3 CIR | 10 | 8 CU | 11:00 AM | 2:00 PM | 3:00 | .02 | SLIGHT | CLEAR, COLD | COLD, SLIGHT SNOW |
| 15 | 70 | 89 | 86 | 0 | 0 | 6 CU | | | | | | MILD, PLEASANT | MILD, PLEASANT |

| | BAROMETER | | | | | | | WIND | | | | | | | | | | |
|---|---|---|---|---|---|---|---|---|---|---|---|---|---|---|---|---|---|---|
| | REDUCED TO FREEZING | | | | | | | DIRECTION | | | MOVEMENT IN MILES | | | | FORCE IN POUNDS PER SQUARE FOOT | | | | |
| DAY | 7 AM | 2 PM | 9 PM | MAXI-MUM | TIME | MINI-MUM | TIME | 7 AM | 2 PM | 9 PM | 9 PM TO 7 AM | 7 AM TO 2 PM | 2 PM TO 9 PM | TOTAL | 7 AM | 2 PM | 9 PM | MAXI-MUM | TIME |
| 10 | 30.388 | 30.342 | 30.300 | 30.390 | 10 AM | 30.294 | 12 PM | N | SE | ESE | 38 | 46 | 62 | 146 | 0 | ¼ | 0 | 1¾ | 8:00 AM |
| 11 | 30.182 | 39.988 | 29.814 | 30.294 | 0 AM | 29.732 | 12 PM | ENE | ESE | ENE | 51 | 82 | 88 | 221 | 0 | 2¼ | 1¼ | 4¼ | 12:00 PM |
| 12 | 29.616 | 29.488 | 29.500 | 29.732 | 0 AM | 29.400 | 12 PM | NNW | NW | NW | 172 | 225 | 239 | 636 | 14¼ | 31 | 18 | 36¼ | 2:15 PM |
| 13 | 29.276 | 29.268 | 29.400 | 29.422 | 12 PM | 29.240 | 10 AM | WNW | NW | NW | 278 | 163 | 149 | 590 | 6 | 10 | 4½ | 15¾ | 1:00 PM |
| 14 | 29.598 | 29.720 | 29.900 | 29.910 | 12 PM | 29.422 | 0 AM | NNW | NNW | NW | 138 | 70 | 76 | 284 | ¼ | 1½ | 3½ | 4 | 0:50 AM |
| 15 | 29.986 | 29.986 | 29.968 | 29.998 | 11 AM | 29.910 | 0 AM | W | NW | WNW | 123 | 87 | 83 | 293 | 0 | 2¼ | ¼ | 3½ | 0:30 PM |

### HOURLY READINGS FROM THE DRAPER SELF-RECORDING THERMOMETER IN THE SHADE
#### FAHRENHEIT DEGREES

| TIME / DAY | 1 AM | 2 AM | 3 AM | 4 AM | 5 AM | 6 AM | 7 AM | 8 AM | 9 AM | 10 AM | 11 AM | NOON | 1 PM | 2 PM | 3 PM | 4 PM | 5 PM | 6 PM | 7 PM | 8 PM | 9 PM | 10 PM | 11 PM | MID-NIGHT | MEAN |
|---|---|---|---|---|---|---|---|---|---|---|---|---|---|---|---|---|---|---|---|---|---|---|---|---|---|
| 10 | 29 | 29 | 29 | 28 | 27 | 27 | 27 | 30 | 34 | 35 | 39 | 42 | 44 | 42 | 43 | 45 | 43 | 40 | 38 | 37 | 37 | 36 | 37 | 36 | 35.6 |
| 11 | 36 | 36 | 35 | 34 | 35 | 36 | 36 | 37 | 38 | 40 | 42 | 42 | 41 | 40 | 39 | 38 | 38 | 38 | 38 | 36 | 35 | 34 | 34 | 33 | 37.1 |
| 12 | 32 | 31 | 29 | 26 | 24 | 24 | 22 | 20 | 18 | 17 | 15 | 14 | 16 | 16 | 15 | 14 | 14 | 12 | 11 | 10 | 10 | 8 | 8 | 8 | 17.2 |
| 13 | 8 | 6 | 6 | 6 | 6 | 6 | 6 | 6 | 6 | 7 | 8 | 9 | 10 | 11 | 11 | 10 | 10 | 10 | 10 | 10 | 10 | 11 | 12 | 12 | 8.5 |
| 14 | 13 | 14 | 17 | 17 | 18 | 19 | 20 | 22 | 25 | 28 | 29 | 29 | 31 | 33 | 34 | 35 | 37 | 36 | 36 | 36 | 32 | 31 | 31 | 31 | 27.2 |
| 15 | 31 | 30 | 30 | 30 | 30 | 29 | 28 | 29 | 32 | 34 | 36 | 36 | 35 | 36 | 37 | 37 | 38 | 34 | 33 | 31 | 32 | 32 | 33 | 33 | 32.7 |

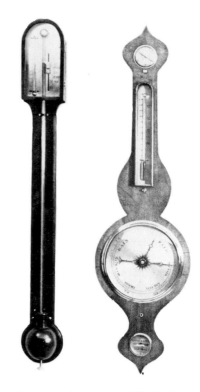

*Barometers by Benjamin Pike & Sons, New York. (The National Museum of American History)*

coming in from the northwest, temperatures recovered to a more seasonable 40°F from Philadelphia to Boston. Skies slowly cleared and, at last, the worst storm ever to hit the northeast was history.

As the storm crossed the Atlantic, its rage intensified again. On March 16 the low that had caused the Blizzard reached Great Britain, downing telegraph wires with a vicious snow storm and gale. Scotland was especially hard hit. From Berlin on March 19, one week after the first snowflakes fell on New York, dispatches reported that northern and eastern Germany were experiencing severe winds and snow. The tempest inconvenienced and delayed European diplomats and heads of state attending Kaiser Wilhelm's funeral. One group of Swedish officials lost contact with their homeland for several days. Disastrous floods caused by heavy rain associated with the same storm wiped out 30 Hungarian villages. Inhabitants struggled to save homes and other buildings as rivers bounded over their banks.

## How Deep Was It?

Precise snowfall measurements after the Blizzard of '88 struck were difficult because of large amounts of blowing and drifting snow. In Hartford, Connecticut, for example, the official record of 19 inches does not

*Recording rain gauge "Jules Richard, Paris"*
*(The National Museum of American History)*

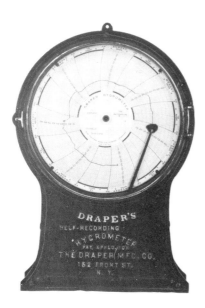

*Draper's Self-recording Hygrometer, New York.*
*(The National Museum of American History)*

*Aneroid Barograph marked "M. Hipp. Neuchâ-*
*tel Suisse 7243." (The National Museum of*
*American History)*

correlate with unofficial observations of three feet and more noted in the local newspapers and in recollections of those who lived through the storm. The Signal Service's weather observer in Hartford took his measurement from the level of snow covering the campus at Trinity College, a hilltop area of several acres with a row of buildings on its western edge. Wind gusts had swept mounds of snow off the campus and deposited them on the steps of hapless homeowners who lived in the Broad Street neighborhood at the bottom of the hill.

On the storm's southern perimeter, the Washington, D.C., area was blanketed by three to six inches of wind-blown snow and ice. Snow accumulations extended as far south as the northern counties of Virginia and the shores of eastern Maryland, Delaware and Virginia. Philadelphia noted ten inches by early morning on March 12, and Atlantic City saw seven inches before skies cleared that afternoon.

Further north, the Blizzard spread little of the brotherly love that had spared Philadelphia from the storm's worst ravages. The recorded snow depths rose dramatically in portions of northeastern Pennsylvania, northern New Jersey, the Hudson River Valley of New York, New York City, Long Island, Connecticut, western Massachusetts, parts of Rhode Island, Vermont and New Hampshire. New York City's official record shows 21 inches, while across the East River, 26 inches buried Brooklyn. Long Island communities were hit with snowfalls measuring anywhere from 18 to 36 inches. An inch short of four feet of snow dumped on Albany, New York, and nearby Troy received 55 inches. Thirty- to fifty-inch measurements were common throughout eastern New York state. While that area was inundated, a sharp dividing line running along a southwesterly path from Plattsburgh near the Canadian border to Scranton, Pennsylvania, separated areas of heavy snow to the east and lighter precipitation to the west.

Throughout western and northern New England, snowfalls were equally dramatic with widespread reports of 20 to 40 inches including 44.7 inches at New Haven, Connecticut, 32 inches at Worcester, Massachusetts, and 27 inches at Concord, New Hampshire. Southeastern New England received huge amounts of precipitation, too, but much of it fell as rain. Boston fluctuated between intervals of rain and wet snow, receiving seven to twelve inches. On Cape Cod, observers noted only a trace of snow, even though the Signal Service watcher at Woods Hole reported the lowest barometer reading associated with the storm.

Most notable about the Blizzard of '88 was the unrelenting intensity of the snowfall. In one 24-hour period, 31 inches of snow fell at Albany, New York. Twenty-eight inches dropped on New Haven, Connecticut, during a similar period. Both snowfalls set records for the greatest amount of snow accumulation over a 24-hour period in both localities. The records still stand today.

The winds whipped the snow into massive drifts wherever it fell. Like Saharan sand dunes, the drifts migrated through open areas until coming to rest as the winds died at the storm's end. Snow piled up to second-story windows in cities and towns throughout the storm's path. The effect was startling in New York City's narrow streets where sidewalks on one side of the street were almost bare but covered with snow 10 to 20 feet deep on the opposite side. In Bangall, a small town in New York's Dutchess County, drift heights ranged from 15 to 40 feet. Cheshire, Connecticut, measured a drift that topped 38 feet. One drift outside of Bridgeport, Connecticut, stood a mere 10 feet tall but stretched almost a mile in length forming a solid wall of snow.

Another startling feature of the snowfall was the way it clung to buildings, trees or anything in its path. From cellar to garret, houses were stuccoed with snow, causing a Manchester, New Hampshire, reporter to remark, "If the icy particles had been fastened on with LePage's glue they could have not stuck more securely."

## A New Ice Age?

Did the storm signal a fundamental change in the climate of the United States? Many who faced what seemed to be an icy apocalypse apparently believed so. General Adolphus W. Greely, chief of the Signal Service, tried to dispel the common misapprehension. The former Arctic explorer assured concerned citizens there were no rational grounds on which to base any statement that the world's climate was changing. While individual months may seem abnormally cold or warm, Greely noted that the century-long records kept by weather watchers in 1888 showed no perceivable trends toward a colder climate. In fact, the ten-year average of temperature for any given month showed only minor and insignificant changes since record keeping began.

Aneroid barograph "Richard Frères" (The National Museum of American History)

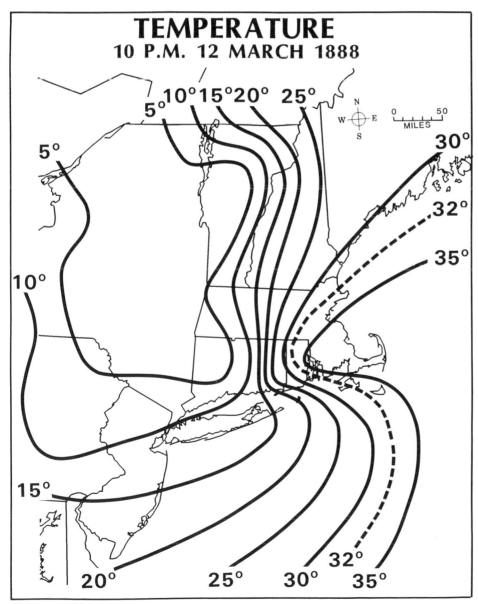

PROVIDED BY PAUL J. KOCIN

Mercury-in-glass thermometers "H.J. Green, Brooklyn, N.Y." (The National Museum of American History)

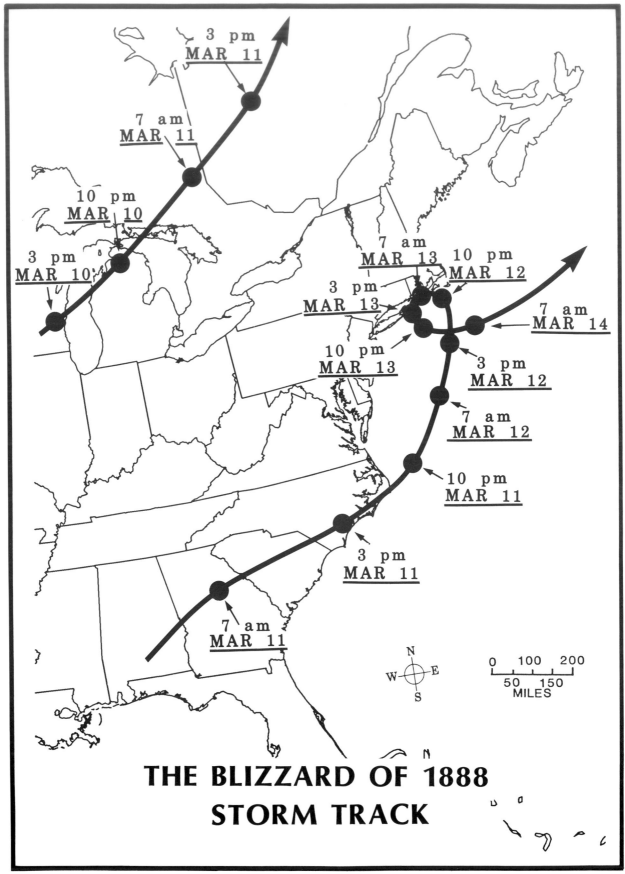

**THE BLIZZARD OF 1888 STORM TRACK**

20

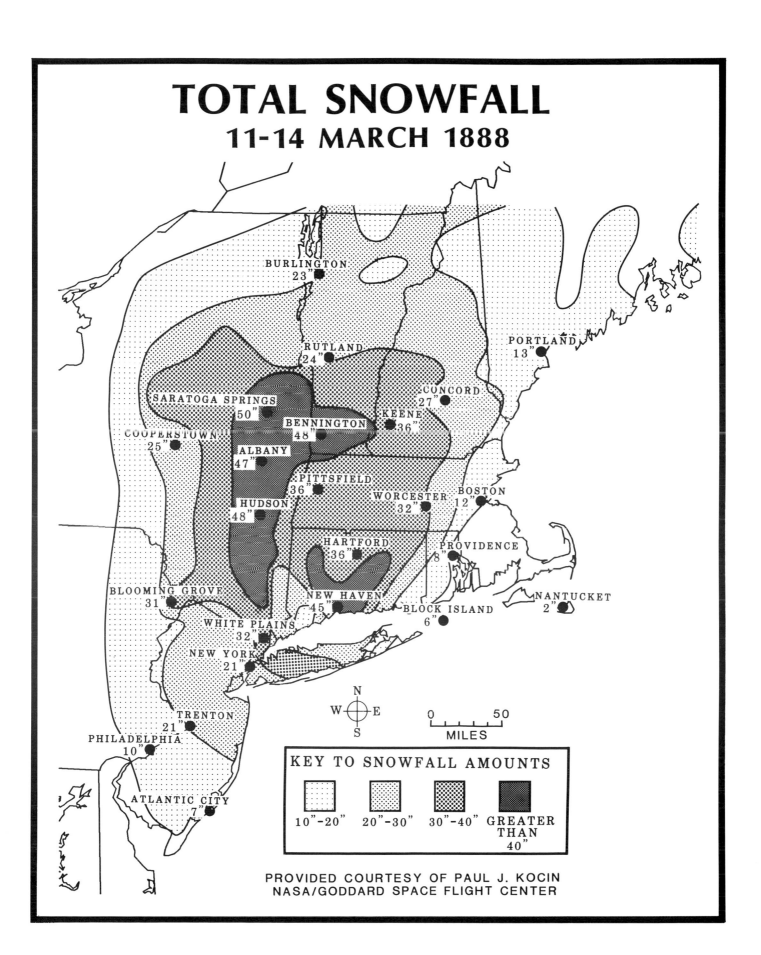

# TOTAL SNOWFALL
## 11-14 MARCH 1888

BURLINGTON
23"

PORTLAND
13"

RUTLAND
24"

CONCORD
27"

SARATOGA SPRINGS
50"

KEENE
36"

BENNINGTON
48"

COOPERSTOWN
25"

ALBANY
47"

PITTSFIELD
36"

BOSTON
12"

HUDSON
48"

WORCESTER
32"

HARTFORD
36"

PROVIDENCE
8"

BLOOMING GROVE
31"

NEW HAVEN
45"

NANTUCKET
2"

BLOCK ISLAND
6"

WHITE PLAINS
32"

NEW YORK
21"

N
W ⊕ E
S

0 — 50
MILES

TRENTON
21"

PHILADELPHIA
10"

ATLANTIC CITY
7"

KEY TO SNOWFALL AMOUNTS

10"-20"    20"-30"    30"-40"    GREATER
THAN
40"

PROVIDED COURTESY OF PAUL J. KOCIN
NASA/GODDARD SPACE FLIGHT CENTER

# SNOWFALL TABLE
## Average Depth of Unmelted Snow, and Total Precipitation

| Station | Est. Snow | Total Precip. |
|---|---|---|
| **W. Virginia** | | |
| Helvetia | 3 | |
| Middlebrook | 8 | |
| | | |
| **Washington, D. C.** | 3 | |
| | | |
| **Maryland** | | |
| Baltimore | 6 | |
| | | |
| **Delaware** | | |
| Dover | 4 | |
| Smyrna | 5 | |
| Wilmington | 8 | |
| | | |
| **New Jersey** | | |
| *Atlantic City | 7 | |
| Belvedere | 24 | |
| Cape May | 10 | |
| Freehold | 20 | |
| Morris County | 20 | |
| Newark | 19 | |
| Newton | 12 | |
| New Brunswick | 24 | |
| Rahway | 25 | |
| Toms River | 24 | |
| *Trenton | 21 | |
| | | |
| **Pennsylvania** | | |
| *Blooming Grove | 31 | |
| Catawissa | 4 | |
| Drifton | 12 | |
| Dyberry | 18 | |
| Easton | 6 | |
| Germantown | 6 | |
| Grampian Hills | 6 | |
| *Philadelphia | 10 | |
| Pittsburgh | 1 | |
| Quakertown | 12 | |
| Reading | 7 | |
| Troy | 1 | |
| Wellsborough | 7 | |
| West Chester | 10 | |
| | | |
| **Eastern New York** | | |
| *Albany | 47 | 3.63 |
| Altramont | 40 | |
| Ballston | 50 | |
| Bangall | 40 | |
| Berlin | 38 | |
| Bolton | 30 | |
| Brooklyn | 26 | |
| Carmel | 30 | |
| Chatham | 42 | |
| Claverack | 48 | |
| Claverack | 34 | |
| Cohoos | 36 | |
| Cold Spring | 48 | |
| Coxsackie | 48 | |
| Croton Falls | 36 | |

| Station | Est. Snow | Total Precip. |
|---|---|---|
| Dover Plains | 39 | |
| Edinburgh | 32 | |
| Elizabethtown | 15 | |
| Hoosick Falls | 42 | |
| *Hudson | 48 | |
| Lebanon Springs | 38 | |
| Mamaroneck | 24 | |
| Middle Granville | 48 | |
| Millerton | 48 | |
| Mt. Vernon | 36 | |
| New Rochelle | 23 | |
| *New York | 22 | 2.46 |
| Palenville | 24 | |
| Patterson | 19 | |
| Pawling | 24 | |
| Peekskill | 26 | |
| Pine Plains | 30 | |
| Poughquag | 30 | |
| Plattsburg | 8 | |
| Rhinebeck | 49 | |
| Rockville | 36 | |
| Sag Harbor | 18 | |
| Sandy Hill | 52 | |
| *Saratoga | 50 | |
| Schaghticoke | 49 | |
| Sharon Station | 20 | |
| Stapleton, S.I. | 24 | |
| Tarrytown | 24 | |
| Towner's | 20 | |
| Troy | 55 | |
| Troy | 46 | |
| Valatie | 48 | |
| Valatie | 42 | |
| Verbank | 28 | |
| Westport | 24 | |
| *White Plains | 32 | |
| | | |
| **Long Island** | | |
| Babylon | 36 | |
| Bridge Hampton | 10 | |
| Flushing | 32 | |
| Glen Cove | 33 | |
| Greenport | 18 | |
| Islip | 29 | |
| Newtown | 10 | |
| Patchogue | 33 | |
| Peconic | 18 | |
| Setauket | 24 | |
| Smithtown | 24 | |
| Speonk | 30 | |
| Springfield | 20 | |
| Westbury | 21 | |
| | | |
| **Interior New York** | | |
| Ardenia - Philipstown | 24 | |
| Auburn | 7 | |
| Boyds Corners | 36 | |
| *Cooperstown | 25 | |
| Factoryville | 3 | |

| Station | Est. Snow | Total Precip. |
|---|---|---|
| Humphrey | 4 | |
| Ithaca | 2 | |
| Menands | 48 | |
| Utica | 35 | |
| | | |
| **Connecticut** | | |
| Ashford | 36 | |
| Barkhampstead | 30 | |
| Branford | 36 | |
| Bridgeport | 18 | |
| Bristol | 38 | |
| Brooklyn | 42 | |
| Canterbury | 14 | |
| Canton | 24 | 1.92 |
| Cheshire | 40 | |
| Colchester | 36 | |
| Colebrook | 36 | |
| Collinsville | 37 | |
| Coventry | 42 | |
| Ellington | 36 | |
| Enfield | 36 | |
| Fairfield | 18 | |
| Falls Village | 34 | |
| Franklin | 24 | |
| Goshen | 43 | |
| Granby | 27 | |
| Groton | 12 | |
| Guildford | 44 | |
| Haddam | 24 | |
| Hamden | 42 | |
| *Hartford | 19 | 2.69 |
| Higganum | 42 | |
| Killingly | 28 | |
| Killingworth | 40 | |
| Lake Konomoc | | 2.17 |
| Lebanon | 36 | |
| Litchfield | 38 | |
| Lyme | 24 | |
| Marlborough | 48 | |
| Middletown | 50 | 5.78 |
| Milford | 24 | |
| New Fairfield | 39 | |
| New Hartford | 42 | |
| *New Haven | 42 | 4.50 |
| New Milford | 27 | |
| Newtown | 24 | |
| New London | 20 | 2.17 |
| North Stonington | 20 | |
| Norwalk | 20 | |
| Norwich | 24 | |
| Plainfield | 20 | |
| Plymouth | 36 | |
| Pomfret | 24 | |
| Portland | 36 | |
| Ridgefield | 19 | |
| Salem | 19 | |
| Saybrook | 36 | |
| Scotland | 20 | |
| Shelton | 25 | |

# SNOWFALL TABLE
## Average Depth of Unmelted Snow, and Total Precipitation

| Station | Est. Snow | Total Precip. | Station | Est. Snow | Total Precip. | Station | Est. Snow | Total Precip. |
|---|---|---|---|---|---|---|---|---|
| Southbury | 36 | 2.27 | Fall River | | 2.86 | Stockbridge | 36 | |
| Southington | 21 | | Fiskdale | 36 | | Taunton | 1 | 2.65 |
| South Manchester | 36 | | Fitchburg | 25 | 2.74 | Taunton | | 1.23 |
| Southport | 36 | | Fitchburg | 25 | 2.38 | Taunton | | 2.48 |
| Thomaston | 42 | | Framingham | | 3.33 | Townsend | 25 | |
| Thompson | 36 | | Gilbertville | 36 | 4.00 | Uxbridge | 20 | |
| Tolland | 36 | | Granville | 36 | | Waltham | | 2.51 |
| Uncasville | 36 | | Greenfield | 34 | | Warren | 36 | |
| Vernon | 39 | 3.26 | Groton | 14 | | Warwick | 36 | |
| Wallingford | 36 | 3.70 | Groton | 31 | 3.52 | Webster | 32 | |
| Waterbury | 42 | | Groton | 13 | | Wellesley | | 3.57 |
| Weston | 18 | 3.55 | Hinsdale | 35 | | Westboro | 24 | 3.00 |
| Westport | 25 | | Holden | 26 | | Westfield | 30 | |
| Westport | 36 | | Lake Cochituate | | 2.77 | Winchester | 12 | 1.92 |
| Willington | 30 | | Lawrence | 14 | | Windsor | 34 | |
| Woodbury | 25 | | Lawrence | 16 | 2.16 | *Worcester | 30 | |
| Woodbury | 30 | | Leicester | 23 | | Wood's Holl | 0 | 1.27 |
| Woodbury | 39 | | Lenox | 29 | | | | |
| | | | Leominster | 18 | 2.77 | **Vermont** | | |
| **Rhode Island** | | | Leominster | 18 | 2.90 | Alburgh Springs | 23 | |
| *Block Island | 6 | 1.00 | Long Plain | | 2.45 | Arlington | 36 | |
| East Greenwich | 6 | | Lowell | 20 | | Barton | 18 | |
| Harrisville | 18 | | Lowell | 18 | 3.70 | Bellows Falls | 32 | |
| Hopkinton | 15 | | Ludlow | 24 | 2.90 | *Bennington | 48 | |
| Kingston | 20 | | Lynn | 10 | 2.95 | Brattleboro | 40 | |
| Little Compton | 1 | | Mansfield | 7 | 3.26 | Brunswick | 24 | |
| Lonsdale | 6 | 2.35 | Mansfield | 38 | 3.16 | *Burlington | 23 | 1.15 |
| Narragansett Pier | 8 | | Marlborough | 15 | | Chelsea | 14 | 1.05 |
| Olneyville | 6 | | Medford | | 1.80 | Chester | 36 | |
| Pawtucket | 8 | 1.77 | Middleboro | 1 | 2.00 | Cornwall | 24 | 2.40 |
| *Providence | 8 | 2.86 | Milton | 7 | 3.30 | Danby | 36 | |
| Providence | 8 | 2.15 | Monson | 39 | 4.25 | Danville | 12 | |
| Westerly | 10 | | Mt. Nonotuck | 32 | 3.65 | Derby | 20 | |
| Woonsocket | 16 | 1.85 | Mystic Lake | | 2.31 | East Charleston | 24 | |
| | | | Mystic Station | | 2.20 | East Dorset | 26 | |
| **Massachusetts** | | | *Nantucket | 2 | 0.68 | Enosburgh Falls | 22 | |
| Amherst | 16 | 3.35 | New Ashford | 36 | | Fairfax | 22 | |
| Ashburnham | 36 | | New Bedford | | 1.45 | Fletcher | 24 | |
| Becket | 36 | | New Bedford | 1 | 1.42 | Glover | 29 | |
| Beverly Farms | 14 | 2.64 | New Braintree | 30 | | Greensboro | 22 | |
| Blue Hill | 9 | 3.07 | Newburyport | 16 | 3.35 | Jacksonville | 40 | 4.13 |
| *Boston | 12 | 2.81 | New Salem | 24 | | Jericho | 18 | |
| Buckland | 30 | | New Salem | 25 | | Leicester | 18 | |
| Buckland | 32 | | Newton | | 2.09 | Lemington | 24 | |
| Cambridge | 12 | 2.34 | North Adams | 40 | | Londonderry | 36 | |
| Cambridge | | 2.37 | Northampton | 34 | 4.68 | Lowell | 14 | |
| Cheshire | 24 | | Norwich | 36 | | Lunenburgh | 24 | 2.40 |
| Chestnut Hill | | 2.59 | Oxford | 30 | | Lyndonville | 18 | |
| Chicopee | 36 | | Petersham | 36 | | Manchester | 24 | 2.40 |
| Chicopee Falls | 36 | | *Pittsfield | 36 | | Marlboro | 40 | 3.61 |
| Clinton | | 1.60 | Plymouth | | 1.30 | Marshfield | 22 | |
| Concord | 24 | 2.85 | Princeton | 30 | | Middlebury | 19 | |
| Cotuit | 0 | 0.89 | Provincetown | 1 | 0.87 | Milton | 20 | |
| Cummington | 39 | | Rowe | 28 | 3.40 | Montpelier | 22 | |
| Deerfield | 24 | 3.20 | Salem | 8 | 2.28 | Newbury | 26 | |
| Deerfield | 27 | | South Egremont | 30 | | New Haven | 30 | |
| Dudley | 36 | 3.50 | South Hadley | 33 | | Newport | 18 | |
| Dudley | 30 | | South Hingham | 2 | 2.10 | Northfield | 27 | 2.22 |
| Easthampton | 34 | | Springfield | 37 | 3.60 | Norwich | 25 | |

# SNOWFALL TABLE
## Average Depth of Unmelted Snow, and Total Precipitation

| Station | Est. Snow | Total Precip. | Station | Est. Snow | Total Precip. | Station | Est. Snow | Total Precip. |
|---|---|---|---|---|---|---|---|---|
| Peacham | 22 | | Haverhill | 20 | | Buckfield | 12 | |
| Peru | 33 | | Hillsborough | 30 | | Bucksport | 14 | |
| Pittsford | 22 | | Hopkinton | 24 | | Calais | 13 | |
| Plymouth | 36 | | Hookset | 20 | | Cambridge | 8 | |
| Poultney | 30 | | Jefferson | 24 | | Camden | 5 | |
| Richford | 15 | | *Keene | 36 | | Castine | 6 | |
| *Rutland | 24 | | Keene | 30 | | Castine | 4 | |
| Ryegate | 24 | | Laconia | 31 | | Corinna | 18 | |
| St. Johnsbury | 27 | | Lake Village | | 3.27 | Dexter | 4 | |
| So. Shaftsbury | 42 | | Lebanon | 24 | | Eastport | 4 | 0.35 |
| Strafford | 20 | 2.00 | Littleton | 18 | | Etna | 15 | |
| Stratton | 42 | | Manchester | 24 | 2.40 | Fairfield | | 0.35 |
| Summerville | 24 | | Manchester | 23 | 2.31 | Fryeburg | 15 | |
| Vergennes | 20 | | Manchester | 21 | 2.05 | Gardiner | 8 | 1.00 |
| Vernon | 38 | 4.35 | Meriden | 36 | | Gorham | 10 | |
| Underhill Centre | 23 | | Milton Mills | 16 | | Greenville | 7 | |
| Warren | 20 | | Nashua | 30 | 3.05 | Houlton | 8 | |
| West Fairlee | 24 | | New Boston | 27 | | Jonesboro | 12 | |
| West Randolph | 28 | | New Hampton | 32 | | Kennebunk | 14 | |
| Woodbury | 15 | | New Ipswich | 34 | | Kent's Hill | 12 | 1.50 |
| | | | New London | 24 | | Lewiston | 14 | 1.43 |
| **New Hampshire** | | | New London | 36 | | Lisbon | 15 | |
| Ackworth | 33 | | North Conway | 15 | 2.00 | Lubec | 18 | |
| Allenstown | 24 | | Ossipee | 24 | | Lubec | 9 | |
| Alton Bay | 18 | | Pittsfield | 24 | | Machias | 12 | |
| Amherst | 36 | | Plymouth | 26 | 4.25 | Mechanics Falls | 16 | |
| Amoskeag Falls | 26 | | Raymond | 18 | | Medford | 6 | |
| Amoskeag Falls | 27 | | Rochester | 22 | | Mercer | 12 | |
| Antrim | 30 | | Rumney | 23 | | Monson | 8 | |
| Atkinson | 24 | | Shelburne | 20 | 1.98 | Monticello | 10 | |
| Atkinson | 30 | | Stratford | 12 | 1.09 | Norridgewock | 8 | |
| Bartlett | 26 | | Suncook | 18 | | Oldtown | 5 | |
| Berlin Mills | 24 | 1.85 | Tamworth | 30 | | Orneville | 8 | |
| Bethlehem | 23 | | Troy | 36 | | Poland | 18 | |
| Boscawen | 24 | | Walpole | 30 | | *Portland | 13 | 0.69 |
| Bradford | 28 | | Walpole | 28 | 2.50 | Richmond | 8 | |
| Campton Village | 20 | | Washington | 36 | | Rockland | 6 | |
| Canterbury | 22 | | Weare | 28 | | St. Albans | 8 | |
| Chesterfield | 40 | 3.85 | West Milan | 17 | | Scarboro | 15 | |
| Claremont | 32 | | West Salisbury | 24 | | Searsport | 4 | |
| Claremont | 36 | | | | | Skowhegan | 9 | 1.80 |
| Colebrook | 24 | | **Maine** | | | Thomaston | 12 | |
| *Concord | 27 | 2.56 | Andover | 14 | | Turner | 12 | |
| Contoocook | 24 | 2.00 | Andover | 18 | | Unity | 12 | |
| Derry | 20 | | Andover | 20 | | Vassalboro | 16 | |
| Dublin | 42 | | Auburn | 10 | | Waterville | 10 | |
| Enfield | 30 | | Augusta | 8 | | Wesley | 16 | |
| Exeter | 18 | | Aurora | 18 | | West Falmouth | 12 | |
| Farmington | 24 | | Bar Harbor | 7 | 0.66 | Whitneyville | 12 | |
| Fitzwilliam | 36 | | Belfast | 6 | | York | 18 | |
| Goffstown | 22 | | Belgrade | 8 | | | | |
| Gorham | 22 | | Biddeford | 18 | | **New Brunswick** | | |
| Grafton | 30 | 3.00 | Bingham | 10 | | St. John | 4 | 0.85 |
| Great Falls | 21 | | Boothby | 20 | | | | |
| Hanover | 25 | 3.00 | Bridgton | 12 | | | | |

Eastern New York, Long Island, the New England States and New Brunswick are from Professor Winslow Upton's tables, reported in the May, 1888 American Meteorological Journal. (Brown University Library)

*Stations on Snowfall Map, of which some amounts have been derived from further research by David Ludlum, Paul Kocin and Judd Caplovich.

# Daily Weather Observations

| Station. | March 12, 10 P.M. | | | | March 13, 10 P.M. | | | |
|---|---|---|---|---|---|---|---|---|
| | Pressure reduced to sea level. | Air Temp. | Wind. Veloc. | Wind. Direc. | Pressure reduced to sea level. | Air Temp. | Wind. Veloc. | Wind. Direc. |
| Eastport, Me. | 29.72 | 30 | 56 | E. | 29.75 | 34 | 30 | E. |
| Portland, Me. | 29.37 | 29 | 31 | N.E. | 29.66 | 33 | 17 | E. |
| Manchester, N.H. | 29.32 | 24 | 15 | N. | 29.62 | 30 | 7 | N.E. |
| Nashua, N.H. | 29.30 | 26 | | | 29.61 | 27 | | |
| Brattleboro, Vt. | 29.51 | 9 | | | 29.64 | 28 | | |
| Northfield, Vt. | 29.76 | 11 | 32 | N. | 29.76 | 13 | 4 | N.W. |
| Blue Hill, Mass. | 29.05 | 32 | 36 | N.N.E. | 29.60 | 24 | 13 | E. |
| Boston, Mass. | 29.09 | 32 | 36 | N. | 29.60 | 30 | 12 | N.E. |
| Nantucket, Mass. | 28.93 | 33 | 12 | S. | 29.56 | 28 | 10 | S. |
| Wood's Holl, Mass. | 28.92 | 35 | 18 | N.E. | 29.55 | 27 | 6 | E. |
| Block Island, R.I. | 29.00 | 29 | 42 | N. | 29.52 | 26 | 24 | S.E. |
| Providence, R.I. | 28.98 | 29 | | N. | 29.53 | 26 | | E.N.E. |
| New Haven, Conn. | 29.36 | 6 | 36 | N. | 29.52 | 23 | 20 | N. |
| New London, Conn. | 29.11 | 25 | 26 | N. | 29.44 | 25 | 6 | N.E. |
| Albany, N.Y. | 29.77 | 5 | 18 | W. | 29.67 | 13 | 10 | N.W. |
| New York, N.Y. | 29.64 | 11 | 31 | W. | 29.61 | 14 | 15 | W. |
| Pilot Boat: Long. 70° 30' Lat. 40° 30' | 29.21 | | | S.W. | | | | |

| Station. | March 13, 7 A.M. | | | | March 14, 7 A.M. | | | |
|---|---|---|---|---|---|---|---|---|
| | Pressure reduced to sea level. | Air Temp. | Wind. Veloc. | Wind. Direc. | Pressure reduced to sea level. | Air Temp. | Wind. Veloc. | Wind. Direc. |
| Eastport, Me. | 29.52 | 32 | 60 | E. | 29.86 | 31 | 18 | N.E. |
| Gardiner, " | 29.37 | 29 | | E. | 29.93 | 34 | | N.E. |
| Portland, " | 29.32 | 32 | 27 | S.E. | 29.82 | 34 | 15 | N. |
| Manchester, N.H. | 29.22 | 28 | 13 | N.E. | 29.79 | 32 | 14 | N.E. |
| Nashua, " | 29.20 | 26 | | | 29.78 | 31 | | |
| Brattleboro, Vt. | 29.31 | 12 | | | 29.81 | 30 | | |
| Northfield, " | 29.54 | 6 | 28 | N.E. | 29.92 | 21 | 2 | S. |
| Blue Hill, Mass. | 29.11 | 22 | 30 | E. | 29.73 | 30 | 17 | N.E. |
| Boston, " | 29.15 | 24 | 38 | N.E. | 29.74 | 33 | 15 | N. |
| Nantucket " | 29.08 | 21 | 27 | S. | 29.71 | 32 | 1 | E. |
| New Bedford, Mass | 28.91 | 24 | | N.E. | 29.67 | 28 | | E.N.E. |
| Newburyport, " | 29.20 | 28 | 22 | E. | 29.78 | 33 | 14 | N.E. |
| Springfield, " | 29.05 | 21 | | N. | 29.72 | 29 | | N. |
| Taunton " | 29.04 | 22 | | N.E. | 29.71 | 31 | | |
| Wood's Holl, " | 28.96 | 22 | 35 | S.E. | 29.70 | 30 | 8 | N.E. |
| Block Island, R.I. | 28.92 | 24 | 36 | N. | 29.70 | 30 | 24 | N. |
| Providence, " | 29.00 | 22 | | N.N.E. | 29.68 | 30 | | N. |
| Middletown, Conn. | 29.21 | 6 | | N.W. | 29.70 | 24 | | N.E. |
| New Haven, " | 29.23 | 7 | | N.W. | 29.74 | 26 | 9 | N.E. |
| New London, " | 29.05 | 14 | 28 | N. | 29.71 | 27 | 4 | N.E. |
| Albany, N.Y. | 29.58 | 2 | 14 | N.W. | 29.85 | 20 | 2 | N. |
| New York, N.Y. | 29.45 | 6 | 37 | W. | 29.75 | 23 | 14 | N.W. |

# Maximum Wind Velocity

| Station | Date, Time | Velocity | Direction |
|---|---|---|---|
| New York | 13, 3:32 A.M. | 50 | |
| New Haven | 12, 3:25 P.M. | 60 | N. |
| New London | 12, P.M. | 46 | |
| Nantucket | 12, 4:30 P.M. | 54 | S.E. |
| Block Island | 12, 11:00 A.M. | 70 | |
| Blue Hill | 12, 5 - 6 P.M. | 57 | |
| Boston | 13, 4:05 A.M. 7:30 | 60 | N.E. |
| Provincetown | 12, 5:00 P.M. | 65 | N.N.E. |
| Portland | 12, 10:02 P.M. | 42 | N.E. |
| Eastport | 13, 6:18 A.M. | 72 | |
| Nashua | 13, | 25 | N.E. |
| Manchester, N.H. | 12, 9:30 P.M. 13, 9:20 A.M. | 28 | N.E. |
| Albany | 13, 3:45 P.M. | 30 | |
| Northfield | 12, 6:46 P.M. | 40 | N. |

Above tables are from the May, 1888 American Meteorological Journal.
(Brown University Library)

*Carriages travel slowly along Broad Street in lower Manhattan after the Blizzard. (The New York Historical Society)*

# Chapter 3 — Chronology of the Blizzard

The Blizzard of '88 affected communities from northern Virginia to southern Maine as it careened up the East Coast. Ferocious winds, driving rain, sleet and snow, and destruction of life and property were its calling cards. Newspaper reports of the day gave a blow-by-blow description of the Blizzard's power.

## The Southern Fringe of the Storm

Foreign invaders could have come ashore at Annapolis or Baltimore during the Blizzard of '88. Officials in the nation's capital would have been unaware and probably unable to do anything about it. Just one telegraph line worked in the city — the underground circuit between the White House and the Capitol. While snowfall in Washington, D. C., was minimal, the high winds caused severe damage and some unusual conditions along the Potomac River. Water levels in the river reached the lowest levels ever recorded. Ferries operating between the city and Virginia communities were high and dry, stuck in the mud on the river bottom without enough water to float. In many places, the river bottom was bare and frozen solid, hard enough to walk across.

Congress continued to plod on despite the storm and communications blackout with the rest of the nation. Debates in the House were dull and mundane, centering on Indian affairs and district matters. In the Senate, silver's role in backing up United States currency was the center of attention.

Between Washington and Philadelphia, however, telegraph and railroad workers were busy clearing the tracks. Telegraph poles, not snow drifts, were the major obstacles. More than 700 poles had toppled in the wind along the railroad link between the two cities, and it seemed that as soon as one was cleared, another pole would fall victim to the gusts just a few yards away. Even with tracks partially clear, passenger trains headed north from Washington had to be cancelled anyway because of a lack of equipment. Most of the rolling stock shuttled between Washington and New York and was imprisoned in deep drifts.

*A derailed engine lists on the tracks in a Newark, New Jersey, freight yard. (The New Jersey Historical Society)*

*A team of horses struggles to pull a coal wagon carrying a half-ton load to a factory in Newark, New Jersey. (The New Jersey Historical Society)*

*These Newark, New Jersey, children moved a lot faster on their sleds than did the passengers of the Pennsylvania Railroad's Chicago Limited hauled by the three locomotives on the opposite side of the fence. The crack express passenger train got mired in a drift shortly after leaving the Newark depot and returned to the station. (The New Jersey Historical Society)*

Philadelphians needed a broom or shovel to find the Monday morning paper on their front steps — if the storm hadn't already blown it to parts unknown. Between Sunday at 11 p.m. and Monday at 6 a.m., Pennsylvania's largest city saw innumerable trees and telegraph poles uprooted, houses unroofed and plate glass windows shattered by the pressure of gale force winds. A thick coating of ice covered anything exposed during the night. By morning, that layer of ice was also blanketed by several inches of snow. Drifts up to six feet high crept down streets and across yards.

By mid-morning on Monday, northbound trains had ceased any attempts to proceed beyond Philadelphia. The Pennsylvania Railroad's Congressional Express took nine hours — triple the usual time — to make the journey from Washington to Philadelphia in the snow. Passengers bound for New York were allowed to stay in relative comfort aboard well-appointed coaches in the station. It would be 48 hours before they moved again.

## New Jersey's Fate

Across the Delaware River in Camden, New Jersey, the situation was no different. Residents found themselves imprisoned in their homes by drifting snow. Ferry operators who were the city's lifeline to Philadelphia found the going hopeless when the combination of severe winds from the northwest and low tide literally blew the water out of the Delaware River. The river levels were so low that loaded boats scraped bottom. At the docks on either side, ferries could not pull into their usual slips. Wagons off the ferries had to be hauled up ice-coated river banks, the horses assisted by rope-pulling men at the dock. At least one ferry went aground in the middle of the channel, stranding passengers between the two ports.

*The top of a broken telegraph pole hangs suspended in midair over a New York City street. The wires held fast to the insulators on the crosspieces, preventing the pole from crashing into the street. (Museum of the City of New York)*

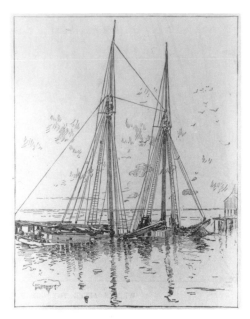

*A capsized schooner succumbs to the tide in Lewes Harbor, Delaware. (Connecticut State Library)*

The low water level in the Delaware caused another problem for residents of Camden. The city took its water supply from the river. Pumps were unable to draw water from the river to reservoirs connected to the city water supply except for an hour or two at high tide. The Pennsylvania Railroad, which normally used Camden's municipal water system to replenish steam locomotives, was forced to juryrig plumbing to dip directly into the river. Other industries, including Camden's local newspaper, were forced to suspend or cut back on work when water needed for steam-powered machinery could not be obtained.

Although spared the worst of the snow, southern New Jersey caught the full brunt of the Blizzard's winds. At Cape May, the snow lasted a mere six hours, but many oceanfront homes were blown apart. A popular resort hotel lost its roof and the brick chimney of the electric generating plant collapsed. Workers in Burlington, New Jersey, looked forward to empty pay envelopes as a result of the storm. The gale force winds first unroofed the Burlington Thread Mill and then caved in the brick front wall causing the entire structure to collapse.

In Newark, New Jersey, a few downy flakes of snow began falling at 11 p.m. on Sunday. A half inch of slush coated the sidewalks by midnight when the temperature started to fall. Throughout the early morning hours, the snow thickened in the air and the wind speed climbed. For the next 24 hours, fine granular snow whirled through the streets until drifts eight to ten feet high completely blocked traffic.

*A coal wagon making a delivery and a horse pulling a sleigh are stuck in deep snow on Thursday afternoon in a residential neighborhood of Newark, New Jersey. (The New Jersey Historical Society)*

At the Singer factory in Elizabeth, New Jersey, about 1,800 of the 3,200 workers made it through the storm to open the plant on Monday morning. By noon, however, it became impossible to keep the steam engines that powered the plant's machinery fed with coal. Plant managers decided to close the facility and send the workers home. Many female

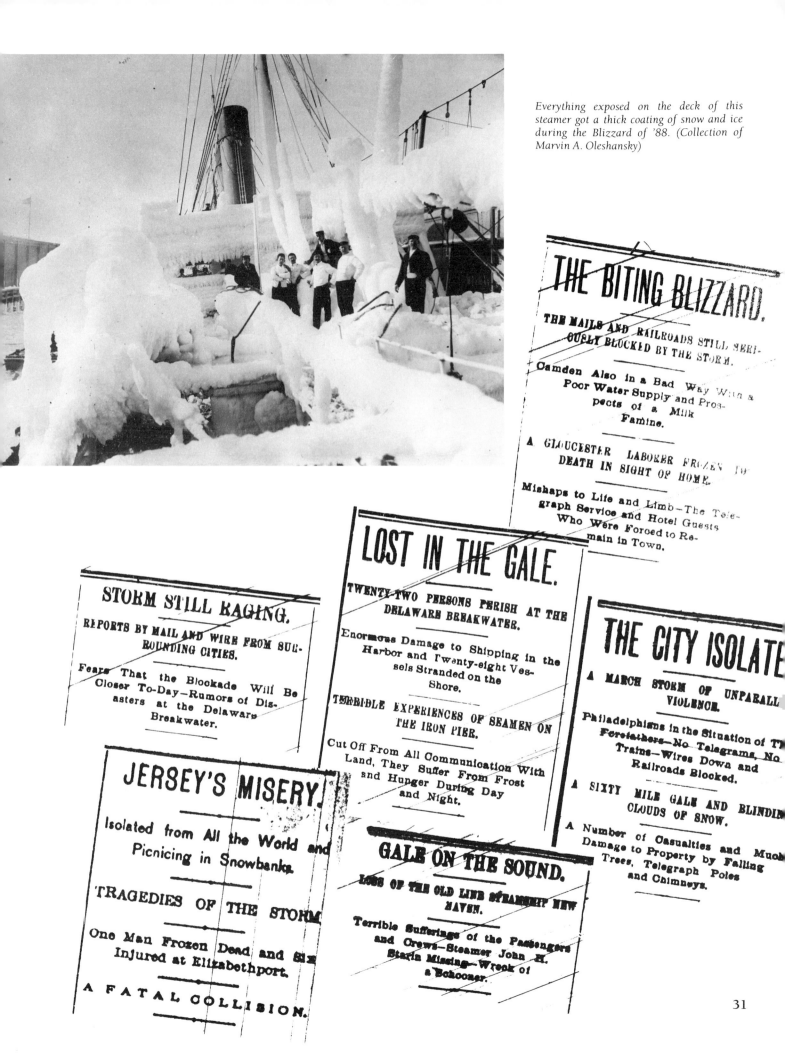

*Everything exposed on the deck of this steamer got a thick coating of snow and ice during the Blizzard of '88. (Collection of Marvin A. Oleshansky)*

## THE BITING BLIZZARD.

### THE MAILS AND RAILROADS STILL SERIOUSLY BLOCKED BY THE STORM.

Camden Also in a Bad Way With a Poor Water Supply and Prospects of a Milk Famine.

### A GLOUCESTER LABORER FROZEN TO DEATH IN SIGHT OF HOME.

Mishaps to Life and Limb—The Telegraph Service and Hotel Guests Who Were Forced to Remain in Town.

## STORM STILL RAGING.

### REPORTS BY MAIL AND WIRE FROM SURROUNDING CITIES.

Fears That the Blockade Will Be Closer To-Day—Rumors of Disasters at the Delaware Breakwater.

## JERSEY'S MISERY.

Isolated from All the World and Picnicing in Snowbanks.

### TRAGEDIES OF THE STORM

One Man Frozen Dead and Six Injured at Elizabethport.

### A FATAL COLLISION.

## LOST IN THE GALE.

### TWENTY-TWO PERSONS PERISH AT THE DELAWARE BREAKWATER.

Enormous Damage to Shipping in the Harbor and Twenty-eight Vessels Stranded on the Shore.

### TERRIBLE EXPERIENCES OF SEAMEN ON THE IRON PIER.

Cut Off From All Communication With Land, They Suffer From Frost and Hunger During Day and Night.

## GALE ON THE SOUND.

### LOSS OF THE OLD LINE STEAMSHIP NEW HAVEN.

Terrible Sufferings of the Passengers and Crews—Steamer John H. Starin Missing—Wreck of a Schooner.

## THE CITY ISOLATE

### A MARCH STORM OF UNPARALLELED VIOLENCE.

Philadelphians in the Situation of The Forefathers—No Telegrams, No Trains—Wires Down and Railroads Blocked.

### A SIXTY MILE GALE AND BLINDING CLOUDS OF SNOW.

A Number of Casualties and Much Damage to Property by Falling Trees, Telegraph Poles and Chimneys.

31

Two engines telescoped into each other at this Flemington, New Jersey, wreck, leaving the tender of the first train atop the second locomotive's boiler. (The New York Historical Society)

Wind-whipped snow hurls past this New York City row house. A drift has crept up the front stairs and halfway up the front door. (The Library of Congress)

employees refused to leave, but most of the men decided to attempt the quarter-mile trek to the railroad station. The workers left the gates in parties of 20 or more, so they could help each other if someone got lost. Kenny Dilts was among them:

> We meant to keep together, but the storm was so terrible that before we were half way we were hopelessly separated. As I went on, I met other men who had gone before. Some were helpless. The face of one was a perfect glare of ice. His eyelids were frozen fast and he was groping blindly along, and as I came up he fell into a drift. I waded up to him, broke the ice from his eyes and tried to rouse him. He was almost in a stupor. I beat him and cuffed him till he recovered sufficiently to struggle on toward the station. I helped four or five men in this way. At last . . . I reached the station. Six men had been terribly frozen on the way. The hands of some of them, the ears of others and even portions of their bodies were frozen. A man named Sherwood had both of his hands frozen to the wrists.

> Behind me, as I afterwards learned, a man named Ellis was picked up out of the snow and breathless. He was carried to the station and died soon afterwards. Two other men were missing from our party. I do not doubt that they are buried in the drifts.

The second day of the storm was election day for many New Jersey municipalities. One candidate for office in New Providence, stranded a few miles from his home, trudged through the drifts on Tuesday morning to make sure that he cast his vote. The effort was in vain; the valiant candidate lost by a single vote.

## New York Confronts The Storm

The gentle rain that splashed New York City's pavement on Sunday turned to wet snow late that evening, filling gutters with slush. The wind began to rise and the thermometer dropped. Suddenly, the whole city gave a shudder as signboards ripped away from moorings and shingles peeled off roofs. But this was only the beginning of the Blizzard's assault on the million inhabitants of America's largest city.

By daybreak, observers could discern only the outlines of thousands of carts abandoned or overturned by the wind in the streets. Butchers and other purveyors, concerned for their own safety, had left their wares without regard for what might happen to their property. Lying across streets and half buried in drifts, butcher wagons piled high with meat, milk trucks crowded with cans, and coal carts lay scattered. Getting anywhere in Manhattan was possible only on foot. The only paths were those worn by thousands of pedestrians walking single file through ravines between the drifts.

Falling awnings, signs, telegraph wires and other debris constantly endangered the lives of those foolhardy enough to tramp through the snow. Littered with the tops of street lights, ornaments from buildings and every imaginable sort of refuse, New York's streets gave the appearance of a war-torn battlefield.

Even birds appealed to human beings for help and shelter from the storm. Hundreds of sparrows flew into the Gilsey House, Hoffman House and other Manhattan hotels. One was said to have perched on the Gilsey House bar for several minutes, oblivious to the crowd that had taken refuge in strong drink during the storm. Thousands more small birds seeking nesting places in trees or on the decorative trim of buildings froze to death and tumbled from their perches to be quickly covered by the snow.

*Drifted snow blockaded steps and entrances to these apartment houses on New York's 114th Street. Doors and first-floor windows on the north side of the street were almost completely covered by drifted snow. (Connecticut State Library)*

*Signs and awnings were ripped from buildings in New York by high winds during the Blizzard. (The New York Historical Society)*

Like the sparrows, thousands of storm-beaten human travelers also besieged Manhattan's hotels. All 450 rooms at the Astor House, one of the city's largest hostelries, were filled by noon, but crowds approached the reception desk late into the night seeking shelter. More than 200 cots were set up in ballrooms, parlors and even bathrooms to accommodate late arrivals. Guests doubled and tripled up in rooms meant for one. One guest whose heart was larger than his room offered to share his quarters with six friends. They had to sleep in shifts. As the day grew long, those without rooms sought refuge on chairs or a few square feet of floor. Hotel managers quickly added surcharges to regular room rates as rooms became scarce.

Rooms were not the only precious commodities. Supplies ran low at many inns. At French's Hotel, 600 refugees crowded into accommodations meant for 200. Many of the rooms were hardly habitable. One man who rented a room early in the day returned to it late that night to find only a bed frame and three slats. A bellhop found another room with a mattress on the bed, but no blankets. The gentleman slept under a single sheet as the cold wind rattled the room's windows.

Justice ground to a halt in the big city. Huge banks of snow blockaded the entrance to City Hall, and no one summoned for jury duty bothered to register. A few clerks put in an appearance at the City Court, but spent much of their time feeding and taming a sparrow that had somehow slipped into the building. Despite the inactivity in the courts, police officers continued to cite and arrest offenders. One was Lawson N. Fuller, whose crime was driving a sleigh on a sidewalk to avoid a drift blocking the street. New York ordinances prohibited such recklessness. The case was thrown out when one of the few judges who managed to arrive at court during the Blizzard refused to believe that the possibility of such an incredible storm had been taken into account when the law was passed.

One long-standing tradition was upheld in New York — the show must go on. Ellen Terry and Henry Irving trekked through drifts from their hotel to the Star Theatre and played *Faust* for a handful of hardy ticket holders. Shakespeare's *A Midsummer Night's Dream* played to about 100 persons at Daly's Theatre. Only two of the roles had to be filled by understudies when actors could not get to the stage. To P. T. Barnum, whose circus had survived six fires, the Blizzard was only a minor inconvenience. At Madison Square Garden, Barnum premiered the spectacle designed ''to astonish the old, bewilder the young, and delight every child in Christendom'' before a crowd of 100.

*Facing page: King Blizzard grips New York in this montage of scenes drawn by Charles Gilbert for* Harper's Weekly. *At top left Wall Street financiers experience the storm's fury. Below, the scene in City Hall Park and abandoned streetcars. At lower right, elevated passengers climb down a rickety ladder. The individual pictures are superimposed over a depiction of hansom cabs trying to navigate through blowing snow and drift-clogged Wall Street in lower Manhattan. (Connecticut State Library)*

*Underwriters for casualty insurers were busy following the Blizzard as storm-related claims poured in. This scene is New York City's Broadway between Liberty and Cortlandt Streets. (The New York Historical Society)*

KING BLIZZARD IN NEW YORK

*Looking for customers after the Blizzard at the Akley Brothers Butcher Shop on Main Street in Hempstead, New York. (Hempstead Public Library)*

Lifesaving crews posted at Coney Island to watch the seas for boats in distress bravely stuck to their duties despite overcoats sheathed in ice and beards stiffened by frost. Housed in a half-buried building on the beach, the crew was witness to an unimaginable scene of destruction. Boardwalks were sucked from their foundations and shattered timbers flew through the air like straws. Mountains of snow drifted against the resort's oceanfront hotels making it impossible to enter or exit except through tunnels bored in the drifts. Like miners, the snow tunnel diggers had to shore up the roofs with scrap lumber to prevent the bulk of the drift from collapsing into the narrow passageway. The storm almost seemed to pick and choose which

*Main Street in Huntington, New York, just after the snow ended. Note the shoveler on the roof of the building at right clearing a drift. (Huntington Historical Society)*

resort hotel would be damaged among the many clinging to the beach. At one a roof would be blown off or a porch collapsed, while the next property would show little or no damage.

*Only sleighs could travel on Main Street in Flushing, New York. (The New York Historical Society)*

Long Islanders knew the Blizzard's fury late Sunday night. By the time residents of Huntington, New York, got up Monday morning, about ten inches were on the ground — and more was coming. It snowed all day Monday and Tuesday, and intermittently on Wednesday and Thursday, making the Blizzard of 1888 the worst snow storm on Long Island since 1719.

*The employees of the Parsons & Co. Marble & Granite Works in Hempstead, New York, take a look at the damage caused by the storm. (Hempstead Public Library)*

37

*Convicts at Sing Sing Prison built a commemorative stove to mark the Blizzard of '88. This 20-inch tall model is now displayed at the Ossining Historical Society.*

Residents of Ossining, New York, got an unruly awakening late Monday night. The snow's weight on the roof of the Arcade File Works was enough to crack open a valve, allowing steam to escape from the boiler. The released steam erupted from the broken valve with a loud shriek, a sound that many residents mistook for the village's fire alarm. A wild chase in the snow ensued as many residents sought out the supposed fire.

*Practical jokers often poked fun at prominent citizens by upending an old pair of pants and boots atop a snow drift. In Ossining, New York, the joke went one step further with a gloved hand and arm sticking out of the side of the drift, too. A sign painted above the effigy reads "DON'T ANKER JOHN ANKER" (Ossining Historical Society)*

*The Blizzard obliterated Washington Square in Troy, New York. (Rensselaer County Historical Society)*

When the storm was over, nearly four feet of snow had crippled Albany, New York. The tempest began as light snow about 8 p.m. on Sunday and continued nonstop for more than 48 hours, bringing business and state government to a complete halt. Both houses of the state legislature adjourned because not enough members could be rounded up for a quorum; only seven senators and nineteen assemblymen answered the roll when Lieutenant Governor Jones gaveled the session to order. Governor Hill transacted the affairs of the state from the executive mansion instead of his state capital office.

*Street clearing crews try to open Washington Street near the state capitol building in Albany, New York. Despite the effort only a few senators and assemblymen answered the roll in the days following the Blizzard. (Albany Institute of History and Art)*

## The Blizzard Hits New England

The snow began falling just after midnight in Bridgeport, Connecticut, 50 miles east of New York City. By dawn, drifts of three to four feet were reported. As afternoon approached, "the snow threatened to obliterate the city" according to an anonymous reporter for the Bridgeport Morning News. Drifts 10 to 13 feet high and more than a mile in length formed by nightfall.

Bridgeport's mills and industrial centers were hit hard by distortions of factory building roofs caused by the sheer weight of the snow. Although mechanical technology had progressed to a substantial point, power for almost all mill machinery still came from a single source such as a water wheel, steam engine or turbines installed in a dam. Equipment received its power through a complex system of overhead shafts, gears and belts hung from the plant's rafters. At the Wheeler & Wilson Manufacturing Company in Bridgeport, a roof deformity caused by the weight of more than a foot of snow destroyed the delicate alignment of the elaborate transmission system. Shafts bent and slipped out of place, gears jammed and ground to a halt, and belts slipped off pulleys making it impossible to power any machinery.

At the nearby Warner Corset Company mill, only 75 out of the 1,100 employees showed up when the factory whistle announced the beginning of the shift. By 9 a.m. the plant's coal supply ran out. High drifts blocking the streets made replenishment by horsedrawn delivery wagons from coal yards unlikely. Workers, dismissed because the factory building could not be heated, were sent out into the streets to fend for themselves in the icy blast.

*Stepping out on a lunch break the day after the Blizzard meant stepping on someone's toes at the corner of Main and State Streets in Bridgeport. With sidewalks narrowed by snow, pedestrian traffic jams were common. (Bridgeport Public Library)*

*"A bit cramped, perhaps, but the price is right,"* a prospective tenant of this snow tunnel in Bridgeport, Connecticut, seems to be saying. (The Connecticut Historical Society)

A few miles to the north in Danbury, Connecticut, light snow began to fall just before Sunday's sunset. Only an inch or so coated the ground by 9 p.m., but by early morning the wind picked up to a violent pace and snow hurled in blinding masses over field and town. The fury of the storm continued unabated on Monday. By noon, drifts of six feet appeared, and in the narrow cuts where railroad tracks pierced the western Connecticut hills, snow piled to a depth of ten feet.

An early shutdown forced The Tweed Manufacturing Company of Danbury to send its workers home when it became impossible to get coal from the bin to the steam engine that powered the plant's machines. A drift blocked the short passage. While most other factories in Danbury, center of the American hat-making industry, closed down, several remained open with workers continuing their tasks rather than chance the arduous journey home.

In the Connecticut city that was the home to Yale University:

Winter saved its best trump for last. A bewildering, belligerent, blinding blizzard . . . it was a corker. If there was ever anything like it before in this part of North America, no one remembers it, and if they did, their testimony against the reputation of this blizzard as the prize storm wouldn't be received. An ordinary storm was to this one like a dew drop to a deluge.

The New Haven, Connecticut, reporter who penned these words didn't know that there were still 24 more hours of snow left to come as he passed in his copy to the editor. Two feet had already fallen by 3 p.m. Monday. Half of that had come down in just 10 hours. The reporter's words would also be the last read by New Haven readers until Thursday when the *Evening Register* published again.

THE AWFUL STORM.

Its Magnitude Never Equalled.

A NIGHT OF HORROR.

All Business Suspended.

Peculiar Street Scenes.

IMPROVISED SNOW SHOES.

The Blizzard struck the Elm City with fury, completely closing down the city by Monday noon. Parents bundled their children and consigned them off to school anyway, only to have them sent home by mid-morning. Teachers and principals organized groups of younger children by neighborhood and charged one or two older students with the responsibility of getting them home safely. Police were ordered to walk their regular beats, but to go indoors and rest for an hour after 90 minutes in the icy blast. The Standard Cab Company, the 1888 equivalent of today's taxi companies, refused all orders for service.

Steamers that normally cruised Long Island Sound between New Haven and New York stayed in port, but the captains and crews of vessels anchored in the harbor's sanctuary could only conjecture about the ugly scenes that must be taking place on those schooners and other ships caught out in open water. Just how many vessels were caught on the Sound was open to conjecture, too. At the lighthouse overlooking New Haven Harbor, life-saving crews could not see ships in distress. The visibility had been reduced to 50 feet or less by the blowing snow. Stores, restaurants and businesses along New Haven's business thoroughfare, Chapel Street, locked their doors by Monday noon. There were no customers. But at the railroad station, business was booming. Hundreds of passengers waiting for connections that never arrived were trapped there. With the station restaurant the only source of food, cooks and waiters worked nonstop to serve patrons. The staff that arrived early Monday morning as the Blizzard began didn't go home until Wednesday night.

Forty-eight hours after a taste of June-like weather had visited Waterbury, Connecticut, the brass mills and machine-tool shops of this industrial center endured the worst storm in many years. Noted a reporter for the city's Monday afternoon newspaper:

> What would have been 15 inches of snow on the level, if it had lain still for a moment, had fallen during the night, but it seemed like about 150 feet when one ventured out. A snowdrift would waltz down the street and strike the earth, then waltz heavenward for a moment, then backward, then forward, now down a man's shirt front, then up his trousers' leg, and finally down the back of his neck. . . . One could easily imagine himself in a vast prairie land and all the horrors of a Western blizzard. . . . The air was dense with the flying particles, making it impossible to tell where the snow on the ground left off and that in the air began.

*Employees of metalworking shops and foundries on Court Street in New Haven, Connecticut, clear the streets to open up a route to their jobs. (New Haven Colony Historical Society)*

# GRIM WINTER.

## The Great Storm and Boston's Isolation.

## Novel Condition of Affairs Yesterday.

## The City Almost Cut Off From the World.

## Experience of Passengers on the Roads.

## Arrival of Several Stalled Trains.

## Severe Sufferings on a New York Express.

By Monday morning snow pelted everything in the city, leaving a sticky residue on the windward side of buildings. Plastered with snow, windows turned opaque. By noon it was impossible to tell where plows had made a feeble attempt to keep streetcar tracks clear. People were few and far between on city streets. For a reporter who walked a few blocks from the newspaper office to the railroad station at mid-morning, the experience was "more terrible than drowning." Going with the wind at the reporter's back was comparatively easy, but the return trip against the icy blast was almost impossible except on hands and knees. When the reporter arrived back at his desk, crusty snow was embedded in his lashes and eyebrows making vision difficult.

A lull in the snow and a thin strip of blue sky seen late Monday afternoon brought false hope to Waterbury residents. Shovelers began clearing sidewalks and removing snow from sagging roofs. But the storm renewed itself shortly after sunset, howling as fiercely as before and obliterating paths dug through the drift. Monday's newspaper was the last issued in Waterbury until Wednesday afternoon. With telegraphic communication at a standstill and no way to verify the rumors of death and destruction that did come in, the publishers of *The American* thought it best to forego publication of Tuesday's edition to avoid alarming readers. Besides, what newsboy would want to hawk papers in such awful weather.

A huge wedge-type snow plow pauses momentarily at the New Milford, Connecticut, depot during cleanup operations after the Blizzard. The plow car was designed to be pushed from the rear by several engines. Despite the massed power, the plow frequently became mired in deep drifts, especially where the tracks ran below grade level. (The Connecticut Historical Society)

This antique oak Detective Camera was manufactured in Waterbury, Connecticut, by the Scovill Manufacturing Company. State-of-the-art equipment at the time of the Blizzard, it produced 4"x5" glass plate negatives. (Jack Naylor Collection)

Throughout the city, startling contrasts in snowfall were created by the mad winds. One homeowner's yard might be buried under six feet, while a neighbor might have a lawn as bare as it might be expected in June. Tunnels through drifts were commonly dug between the street and store entrances. Men, desperate to get to factory jobs, tied boards to their feet as crude snowshoes. Scovill Manufacturing, one of the town's largest employers, had to close when snow blocked a ditch that diverted water from the Naugatuck River to the plant. School entrances were blocked by drifts up to 15 feet high; board of education officials didn't expected them to re-open for at least a week. In one unusual incident, a dog lover prodded a reluctant Newfoundland to relieve himself along the drifts on Central Avenue. Suddenly, the immense mutt sank from view. Minutes later, the canine emerged down the street after tunneling through the snow like a miner with his huge paws.

In nearby Meriden, Connecticut, light snow was reported at 5 p.m. on Sunday. By early Monday morning, trains were stuck at the fringe of town on both ends of the railroad line, effectively blocking all railroad traffic in and out of the city.

Hartford's precipitation began early Sunday night with the mercury hovering around 40 degrees. A lull in the storm at midnight left some thinking that only a few inches of snow would fall. Just after 2 a.m. "it began with a violence, the snow coming in blinding sheets and the wind blowing with fury which increased during the day," according to the *Hartford Courant*. By Monday at 10:30 a.m., more than two feet of snow had fallen on Hartford's downtown streets. Shovel brigades that tried to keep up with the accumulation had difficulty; new snow covered paths as fast as it could be removed. The snow fell unabated until late Monday night. The respite was brief as the snow started again with a vengeance at 5 a.m. on Tuesday, leaving behind an unofficial total of 36 inches and drifts as high as 12 feet when it finally ended Tuesday night. The gale force winds kept attempts to clear the snow at bay by piling up new drifts as soon as old ones were removed.

Hotels crowded with involuntary guests, including one Hartford businessman who offered hack drivers $50 for the one mile ride to his house but found no takers. Hunt, Holbrook & Barber put up their 25 women employees in the Park Central Hotel, but most workers stuck at their jobs used factory and shop floors as makeshift sleeping quarters. The Plimpton Manufacturing Company tried sending its employees home by sleighs early Monday afternoon, but none could be procured. Roped together like Alpine climbers, eight women employees followed a male co-worker who broke a path leading to homes and safety.

The 500 men who reported for work at Pratt & Whitney the day after the storm found themselves with an additional job responsibility. After running the plant for about two hours, word spread that the coal supply was running out — the factory normally consumed seven tons a day to run its machinery. A shutdown and temporary layoff of workers would ensue unless something could be done. Workers wanted to be able to earn their pay. Management wanted to keep the plant open. A firm bed of snow on the streets would enable coal wagons to transport fuel to the plant. So, minutes later, workers poured out of the factory gates with their new task. Five hundred pairs of heavy work boots stomped down the snow on the streets that led from plant to coal yard.

The procession was soon joined by 200 men from the nearby Weed Sewing Machine and Hartford Screw Company plants. Like Pratt & Whitney, both had been forced to close when the coal supply for steam-powered machinery ran out. With plant foremen at the head of the line, the workers stamped out a path more than a mile long to reach the coal yards. Anxious to get back to work, workers loaded a massive sled with two tons of coal. Pulling long ropes, the workers towed the loaded sled back to the plants. The entire operation took just three hours to complete.

*Hundreds of employees from Pratt & Whitney stomp down the snow on Hartford's Capitol Avenue To keep the factory running, the workers smoothed down a mile-and-a-half-long path from coal yards by the Connecticut River to the factory gates to bring sleds laden with coal to the plant. (The Connecticut Historical Society)*

Torrington, Connecticut's weekly newspaper noted that the wind "was a constant undertone — a horrible, never-ceasing roar, covered with recurring, prolonged shrieks as the furious blasts put forth their full strength." In homes and businesses "snow sifted into every crack and between window casings, and in some houses it had to be carried out of rooms by hod-fulls." During the night the wind rose to a furious pace. Sleep was difficult as many persons wondered if the roof would hold in the wind. Chimneys collapsed under the stress of the wind including one at the city's electric generating station, which destroyed the main electrical feeder lines and plunged homes and businesses that used Edison's recent invention into darkness.

## Massachusetts Bears The Brunt

Snow started falling in Springfield, Massachusetts, at 9:30 Sunday evening, and by dawn ten inches covered the ground. Drifts five feet high formed as high winds blew snow into the entrance of the railroad depot. Horsecar lines were abandoned early. There was some attempt by the horsecar company to provide alternate transportation with sleighs, but even this effort had to be halted by Monday noon.

*Drifts sweep up toward buildings on the north side of Asylum Street in downtown Hartford.(The Connecticut Historical Society)*

*A westbound train on the Connecticut Western Railroad bucks a huge drift near Norfolk, Connecticut. (The Connecticut Historical Society)*

*Horsecars, like this one marooned on Main Street in Springfield, Massachusetts, littered the streets of many cities struck by the Blizzard. Frequently, drivers would leave passengers to fend for themselves when cars got mired or went off the tracks. (Springfield Public Library)*

47

*Muscle power was the only way to move the snow in many places. More than 100 workers were used to clear the tracks of the New York, New Haven & Hartford railroad near the Hollow Tree Ridge Road overpass in Darien, Connecticut. The supervisor is leaning against the telegraph pole at right. (Darien Historical Society)*

William E. Sikes was a ten-year-old boy living in West Springfield at the time of the Blizzard. Years later, he told this story to his niece:

That evening of March 11, we were sitting in the large kitchen reading and enjoying some popcorn when around nine o'clock Henry Dewey . . . arrived to pick up the newspaper which we usually passed along to him. I heard him say "It's snowing a little," a remark that turned out to be the understatement of the century as far as snowstorms in New England are concerned.

We retired that night as usual and when I arose the next morning, the wind was rising and the fast falling snow was swirling about and piling up in drifts everywhere. All that forenoon the storm continued and, as the time came, toward midday for watering the livestock from a large tub in the barnyard, it was with great difficulty that the cattle made the trip and back to the stable again. I had never seen it storm harder. The howling wind sent the fast falling snow slithering off the big barn roof so that by night it was plain to see that it would be impossible to water the cows on the morrow in the usual way.

By noon the snow had already reached the window sills of the ell of the house and was gradually and relentlessly climbing higher. By mid-afternoon, I recall, my mother was walking back and forth in the house, stopping now and then to peer through the fast disappearing window panes.

All that night the the storm raged and when we arose on Tuesday morning it was the snowiest looking landscape that I have ever seen. Due to some freakish wind currents, there was scarcely any snow close to the big barn doors, but just a few feet back was a giant drift many feet deep. . . .

The four stable doors along the east side of the barn next to the barnyard were covered to the tops including all the windows along that side so that we had to use lanterns to do the morning milking.

At the front of the house was a towering drift that was up to the top of the first story windows. It was below my bedroom and later that day I went up-stairs and jumped from the window sill into it. I landed safely enough but I found myself completely buried under the white blanket and I had quite a struggle getting out of it and into the house again. There was a little used out-side door in the kitchen . . . when this was opened on Tuesday morning only a white wall was revealed, as the snow was level with the eaves of the one story ell on that side of the house. Later on, as the snow settled, my sister would open the door and set the molasses candy out on the drift to cool.

AN UNWILLING DR. TANNER.

In Worcester, Massachusetts, snow arrived Sunday night at 11:15 p.m. and continued nonstop until Tuesday. The *Worcester Daily Telegram* estimated the total snowfall at two feet, "but the boisterous wind piled it up in great drifts, mountains high, and unless one looked sharply, he was apt to find himself wallowing in snow that consorted with his middle waistcoat buttons."

Officials correctly estimated the severity of the storm in this central Massachusetts community shortly after flakes began to fall. The no school signal sounded from bells throughout the city in the early morning hours, causing children to rejoice at the prospect of a holiday. Their joy redoubled at noon when the signal rang out indicating that classrooms would close again on Tuesday. Principals weren't so lucky. School board regulations required them to be in attendance no matter what the weather might be.

"CUT OFF"

This two-word bold headline in the *Boston Globe* tersely described the situation on March 13 in New England's largest city. The storm as it passed through demonstrated Mark Twain's familiar comment on New England's weather — "If you don't like the weather, wait a minute!" Sunday's twilight was dull and gray, and rain soon began to fall. A blinding snowfall accompanied by winds that gusted to 50 miles per hour engulfed Boston by 7 a.m. on Monday. In the span of 18 hours, the barometer dropped more than an inch. Snow alternated with rain and sleet throughout the day.

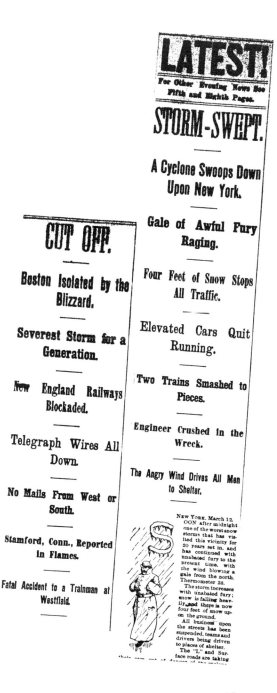

**LATEST!**

For Other Evening News See Fifth and Eighth Pages.

**STORM-SWEPT.**

**A Cyclone Swoops Down Upon New York.**

**CUT OFF.**

**Boston Isolated by the Blizzard.**

**Severest Storm for a Generation.**

**New England Railways Blockaded.**

**Telegraph Wires All Down.**

**No Mails From West or South.**

**Stamford, Conn., Reported in Flames.**

**Fatal Accident to a Trainman at Westfield.**

**Gale of Awful Fury Raging.**

**Four Feet of Snow Stops All Traffic.**

**Elevated Cars Quit Running.**

**Two Trains Smashed to Pieces.**

**Engineer Crushed in the Wreck.**

**The Angry Wind Drives All Men to Shelter.**

New York, March 12. — Soon after midnight one of the worst snow storms that has visited this vicinity for 20 years set in, and has continued with unabated fury to the present time, with the wind blowing a gale from the north. Thermometer 28.

The storm increases with unabated fury; snow is falling heavily, and there is now four feet of snow upon the ground.

All business upon the streets has been suspended, teams and drivers being driven to places of shelter.

The "L" and Surface roads are taking

*Pedestrians in New York City's Union Square hold on to their hats and each other as they battle the fierce winds. (Connecticut State Library)*

As the wind shrieked down chimneys of the brick townhouses on Beacon Hill, few suspected the damage being wrought by the Blizzard in other localities surrounding Boston. Very little news managed to penetrate the storm-enforced blockade. The wharves in this busy seafaring town had a desolate appearance. Few ships entered and none left the harbor.

In coastal communities north and south of Boston, the scene was one of desolation. Wave after wave crashed against piers, cottages and ocean-front resort hotels. Railroad tracks parallel to the shore about 10 miles north of the city were washed out, stranding a passenger train. Waves breaking over the bulkhead in front of the Vue de l'Eau Hotel in Crescent Beach completely enveloped the structure. The hotel quaked like an aspen leaf in the wind with each salt water onslaught.

*Crowds gather to peer in wonder at the first train to arrive in Hartford from the south after the Blizzard. Windows in the cab were completely clogged with snow, preventing the engineer from seeing where he was going. (Archives, History and Genealogy Unit, Connecticut State Library)*

## Up North

Snow started falling on northern New England communities late Sunday night and continued almost without interruption until Wednesday. Peterborough, New Hampshire, was cut off by 2 p.m. on Monday when all railroad traffic ceased. The shoe factories on which the town's economy depended operated through the Blizzard with only skeleton crews; most of the regular laborers gave up trying to battle the elements on Monday morning. A few miles away in New Hampshire's state capitol of Concord, gale force winds whipped the snow, blockading the city by nightfall.

"It was a day when the small boy who expected to shovel off the sidewalk in front of the paternal mansion gazed dubiously down on the accumulating drift, when every lucky individual in comfortable quarters smiled a huge smile of satisfaction, and every unfortunate, whose calling caused him to stand up and face the icy blast for hours, thought gloomily of his hard fate, and sighed for kind fortune to come to his relief," said a reporter who covered the storm for Manchester's *New Hampshire Union*.

For New Hampshire towns, the second Monday of March was the day when annual town meetings were mandated by state law. Established in colonial times as a way to get all landowners involved in matters of local government, the town meeting set the town's budget and tax rates for the coming year. It afforded a chance for citizens with problems or concerns to confront town leaders. Political parties held caucuses to select candidates for town offices. Usually these meetings lasted well into the night with the women of the town preparing pot luck refreshments for all to share. In addition to the stated purpose of making democracy work in rural New England, the town meeting served as the entertainment event of the season, a chance to catch up on news from neighbors and friends who were less accessible during the winter months.

REMOVING THE DRIFTS.

*Gaudy signs hawking businesses along Manchester, New Hampshire's Hanover Street offer a sharp contrast to the mound of snow blocking the street. (Manchester Historic Association)*

In 1888, town meeting day happened to fall on the day of the Blizzard. Despite the attractions of these local meetings, attendance was poor. Town clerks who struggled through the gale to the meeting houses and churches where the gatherings were held found quorums difficult or impossible to attain. Most meetings were adjourned and postponed to the following week.

In Tilton, New Hampshire, barely a third of the 429 registered voters participated in the town meeting; most came from the village surrounding the meeting house. George H. Brown, cited by the town clerk as the bravest voter in Tilton, had trekked three miles on snowshoes to attend the affair. Men at Hudson's town meeting were obliged to spend the night on the hard pews in the village's church where the meeting was held. One farmer who journeyed from an outlying part of town said the snow was so deep that only the back of his horse could be seen as he plunged through the deep snow.

In the hills of southern and central Vermont, snow fell without letup from about 6 p.m. Sunday until Wednesday afternoon. By Tuesday morning in Bellows Falls, houses were nearly covered by drifts. All windows were blocked and only the roof peaks were visible. The front door of the town's only hotel was barricaded by a two-story drift. The only access was a narrow tunnel dug by hotel employees. Drifts 15 feet high crippled the state capital of Montpelier. Monday's express train from Boston arrived exactly at the scheduled time, just one day late.

The fierce north wind drove snow almost horizontally down Main Street in the Connecticut River town of Brattleboro located in the southern part of Vermont. The air was so thick with snow that the eye could not make out the outlines of buildings less than 100 feet away. A doctor summoned on Monday night to deliver a baby in West Brattleboro, three miles from his Main Street office, didn't return to town until late Tuesday afternoon. Mother and child came through in fine shape, but the doctor's sleigh got stuck in a snow drift. After remaining with the family through the night, the physician spent the next day finding his way home through the white desert of the storm's wake.

*Postman Spencer W. Knight made his rounds in Brattleboro, Vermont, after the Blizzard. The mail sack wasn't very heavy this day — most mail was still aboard stalled trains or in the originating post office waiting for a departing train. (Brattleboro P.H.O.T.O.S.)*

# Chapter 4 — How the Storm Affected People

To gauchos of the Argentine pampas who must face the blasts of the southern hemisphere's winter, the word for blizzard is *el tormento*. No word better speaks of the anguish felt by those who experience it.

Blizzards can obliterate the closest, most familiar landmarks. Snow falls so thickly and furiously that it's almost impossible to breathe without sucking in a suffocating breath. If the temperature is low, the snow tends to be fine and sifts through minute crevices between windows and frames or under doors. At slightly higher temperatures, the snow turns wet and even a relatively thin blanket can cave-in roofs and walls. The combination of wind and wet snow can encase unprotected eyes and nostrils like plaster.

The suffering and hardships associated with a blizzard can be dreadful, yet a blizzard need not be dangerous even for someone stranded in it. Eskimos and polar explorers have survived brutal storms by remembering not to fight the storm foolishly — a rule many either didn't know or chose to ignore during the 1888 storm.

Industrial workers had good reason to battle the '88 Blizzard to reach factories or offices. In those days, job protection was virtually unheard of. A laborer who spent a day off the job was likely to return and find the position filled by someone else willing to work at a lower rate of pay. In urban centers along the east coast, a huge influx of European immigrants — willing to take any job at almost any rate of pay — insured that employers had an ample supply of labor. Absence from a day's work also meant the loss of a day's salary; there were no provisions for paying employees who failed to show up, no matter how convincing the reason. For many laborers, a day's pay meant the difference between eating and going hungry that week.

Many workers who struggled through the storm found themselves in the same position as William Scribner of Cannondale, Connecticut, a wire weaver at the Gilbert & Bennett Manufacturing Company. Scribner walked the mile from his house to the mill every working day. On the first day of the blizzard, as he staggered toward the main gate, he heard the morning whistle blow marking the start of the shift. When he was just a few steps

A Southington, Connecticut, resident gets a rare perspective of Center Street. (Barnes Museum, Southington)

from the entrance, the guard locked the gate. Despite the storm, management considered Scribner to be just another late employee and docked him a day's pay. Neither he nor his co-workers dared question the system under which the mill was run.

Rural folks had a distinct advantage over their city cousins. Those who lived on farms were used to heavy storms and far more prepared to deal with them. While city dwellers faced cold hungry nights when larders ran low and no supplies could be gotten from the neighborhood grocery, country people had stocks of canned goods, cured meats, and ample supplies of flour and other provisions for baking. Rural inhabitants frequently were the first to reach stranded trains with supplies of food baked in their own kitchens. Some generous individuals distributed food without charge to stalled passengers, but many more seized the opportunity to make a fast buck by charging exorbitant prices for small portions.

## The Icy Fingers of Death

The Blizzard of '88 brought death to an estimated 400 individuals during its fury and aftermath. The storm did not discriminate against anyone. Men, women and children were its victims. Young and old, strong and weak, the rich and the homeless succumbed to its deathly grip. City streets, country fields and ships at sea served as temporary graves for the unlucky ones. Thousands of others narrowly escaped death and suffered the after-effects of exhaustion and frostbite.

*Below and facing page: Telegraph and telephone wires droop low on Wall Street as two men face the icy blast holding their hats and covering their ears to protect against frostbite. Compare the scene below with the photograph on the opposite page depicting the heart of New York's financial district without snow on a typical day in the mid-1880s. The photographs were taken from vantage points less than a block apart. (The New York Historical Society)*

For days following the tempest, storm-related deaths were announced in the obituary columns. Those who ventured out of doors at the height of the Blizzard frequently lost their way and strayed from streets, sidewalks and paths. Some gave up to fatigue; others ranted against the snow, screaming about the agony of their fate. Deep drifts and the intense snowfall quickly buried tired travelers who fell unconscious from injury, exhaustion or frostbite. If a body lay where post-storm clearing was not essential, discovery came only as melting snow uncovered a limb or article of clothing. For several days after the storm, newspapers carried single-paragraph stories about missing persons found frozen in snow drifts. Those who perished at sea washed up on shore days later and miles from where their ships were sunk or overcome by the storm.

The Blizzard's best-known casualty was also one of its last — Roscoe Conkling. The former U.S. Senator, aspirant to the White House and New York Republican Party kingpin, Conkling is traditionally counted among the storm's victims although his actual death did not occur until April 18, some five weeks after the snowfall.

Dr. Fordyce Barker, Conkling's attending physician from April 2 until his demise, lists the cause of death as "acute otitis media and suppurative inflammation of the mastoid cells with pulmonary edema," complications of exhaustion and exposure to the elements brought on by walking from his downtown Wall Street office up to midtown Manhattan during the height of the storm.

**FINDING THE BODY OF GEORGE D. BAREMORE IN A SNOWDRIFT ON SEVENTH AVENUE.**

*One of those who tried to get to work on Monday morning was George Baremore, a merchant who dealt in malt and hops. Departing on foot from his exclusive Manhattan apartment at the corner of 57th Street and Seventh Avenue, Baremore underestimated the power of the storm and attempted the arduous journey to his Water Street office. Finding the Sixth Avenue elevated station closed, Baremore tried to walk three blocks to the Ninth Avenue line. A victim of chronic asthma and subject to fainting, he collapsed in a snow drift near 54th Street and Seventh Avenue. Soft snow quickly buried him. Hours later, patrolmen Louis Graf and Henry Haag accidentally stumbled on his frozen body. This illustration from* Frank Leslie's Illustrated News *depicts the grim discovery.*

"Roscoe Conkling said yesterday that he has a pretty tough constitution and had been in some pretty tight places in his life, but he had never found himself as far gone physically as on Monday night in Union Square," reported William A. Hoy, who interviewed Conkling for the *New York Sun* just after his ordeal.

A Wall Street lawyer, the robust 59-year old senator neither smoked nor imbibed and kept in top physical shape by boxing regularly at a nearby gym. Conkling worked through the first day of the Blizzard, but when he decided to go home at 6 p.m., he found himself stranded without a cab or carriage in sight. Heading uptown on foot in the darkness of storm-ravaged Manhattan, the senator at one point found himself trapped up to his shoulders in a snow drift. For 20 minutes Conkling struggled and finally pulled himself out of what could have been an icy tomb. Arriving at the New York Club at the upper end of Madison Square after three hours in the Blizzard, a hefty walk even in the best weather, he collapsed in the lobby.

William Sulzer, a young lawyer who occupied an office adjacent to Conkling's, had suggested to the senator that they should stay in their offices for the night to wait out the storm. Conkling, described as a "big, strong, robust man" in Sulzer's account, insisted that they could walk uptown to his hotel.

"We started up Broadway full of determination to get home," Sulzer notes, "but the snow banks were so big, and the storm so great, that we had great difficulty in making progress. The senator kept a bit ahead of me, and urged me to follow in his footsteps.'' Sulzer sojourned with Conkling as far as the Astor House Hotel on the corner of Broadway and Vesey Street and decided to spend the night there while Conkling continued on alone.

The decision to seek shelter and wait out the Blizzard proved to be a wise one for Sulzer. Unlike Conkling, the young lawyer suffered no ill effects from his struggles. In coming years, Sulzer was to rise through the ranks of New York's political machine and become the state's governor in 1912.

Conkling's struggle through the mountains of snow in Manhattan got nationwide publicity in the newspapers of the day. After reading the wire service account, A. W. Edwards, editor of the *Fargo* [Dakota Territory] *Argus* telegraphed best wishes and a ribbing to the ailing senator:

> The Dakota robins, sitting on orange trees, in blossom, join in thanks for your safe delivery from New York's snowdrifts . . . all join with me in congratulations to you and say: 'Come to the banana belt, where every man is your well-wisher.'

Whether Conkling enjoyed the telegram's humor is not noted. The obituary in the *New York Times* indicated that Conkling stubbornly refused to follow his doctor's advice when he became ill. Five weeks after the Blizzard, Conkling was buried in Utica, New York.

# BLIZZARD WAS KING

## The Metropolis Helpless Under Snow.

## HARDLY A WHEEL TURNS

### Business Knocked Flat as if by a Panic.

### PLAYS, TRIALS, FUNERALS, ALL POSTPONED.

### Fifty Train Loads of Passengers Stuck on the Main Lines.

### WHERE THEY ARE, HEAVEN KNOWS.

### A Wonderful Change in Our Ways of Living and Moving Sprung on Us in a Night

### ELECTRIC LIGHTS OUT.

### MIGHTY LITTLE NEWS GOT INTO TOWN OR GOT OUT OF IT.

### GOING TO LET UP NOW

### The Elevated Roads After a Day's Paralysis Get a Half Hold Again on Travel.

*The Blizzard wasn't child's play, even if your beat did include Crandall's Toy Store. Here a well-bundled Brooklyn police officer grimaces at the snow. (The Library of Congress)*

*Abandoned streetcars sit idle near the corner of State and Union Streets in Springfield, Massachusetts. (Springfield Public Library)*

*Stuck in the snow, a forsaken horsecar sits in the middle of Main Street in Springfield, Massachusetts. (Springfield Public Library)*

Conkling was the storm's most prominent victim, but dozens of other stories are told about how persons met their doom in the icy clutches of wind and blinding snow.

Two Bridgeport, Connecticut, women, apparently more concerned about Victorian moral standards than their own safety, resisted the advice of their male foreman, who urged them to spend the night in the cartridge factory where they worked. Braving the storm and walking home Monday evening, they were enveloped by wind-driven snow as they passed through the factory gate. Workers digging a path on Wednesday morning found the pair frozen to death in a snow drift a few yards from the factory gate, locked in each other's arms. High winds caused another death in Bridgeport, when a railroad signal tower was blown down. An employee stationed in the tower was crushed and several others working with him were injured.

58

Staying overnight at a friend's home on New York City's 96th Street, Nancy Sankey-Jones recalled the horror of watching from a window one man's losing battle against the winds and snow.

I saw a man for one and a half hours trying to cross 96th Street. We watched him start, get quarter way across and then flung back against the building on the corner. The last time he tried it, he was caught up in a whirl of snow and disappeared from our view. The next morning seven horses, policemen and his brother charged the drift and his body was *kicked* out of the drift.

Arriving at her own home the following day after a strenuous eight-block walk, Miss Jones made her entrance through a second-story window. The front door was completely blocked by a drift.

Two days after the storm in New Brunswick, New Jersey, a farmer shoveling a path on his property made a grim discovery — the body of a woman who had frozen to death in his outhouse. The woman had last been seen on Monday walking along a road near the farm and apparently had gone into the shack to seek shelter from the biting wind.

Many persons barely escaped death. When Edwin F. Leonard of Springfield, Massachusetts, reached to pick up a hat lying atop a snow drift, he found an unconscious young girl completely buried in the snow. Using only his bare hands in a fit of frenzied digging, Leonard managed to free the girl and carry her to shelter. She was revived and recovered with few ill effects. Telegraph boys, charged with the delivery of the few messages that managed to get through the tangle of downed wires, rummaged through the store rooms of Western Union offices looking for wire to wrap around their waists. Should they became bogged down in snow, the wire belts would provide something for rescuers to grab.

*The first commercially produced hand-held instantaneous camera in the United States was Schmid's Patent Detective Camera. Its small size and ability to produce images without bulky tripods or long exposures made it a favorite among candid photographers around the time of the Blizzard. The photos on the opposite page were probably taken with this or a similar camera. (Jack Naylor Collection)*

*Persons who could not get home from work often sought out shelter in hotels. The men who stayed at Cooley's Hotel in Springfield, Massachusetts, posed for this photograph. (Springfield Public Library)*

*Snow crews working from the opposite ends of Main Street in Poughkeepsie, New York, meet at a tunnel excavated in a drift at Main and Little Smith Streets. One wonders if a "golden shovel" might have been used to toss the last load of snow. (Dutchess County Historical Society)*

The storm forced funeral directors in many areas to take a holiday. Winds and blowing snow made it impossible to dig graves or conduct burial services. Gravediggers at one New York burial ground gave up when snow drifted into newly dug plots as fast as it could be shoveled out.

"A funeral started out yesterday afternoon for one of the outlying cemeteries," said Dr. Metcalf of the New York City Health Department to a *New York Herald* reporter. "Despite the efforts of the undertaker to whip up his horses, it was impossible to get to the cemetery. He was literally stuck. The hearse containing the body was drawn to the side of the road, the horses were unhitched, and for the next few days that funeral will be postponed." The ghastly scene was repeated throughout the storm-affected area.

In Waterbury, Connecticut, the funeral of Mrs. Edwin Tolles, who died on Saturday, was postponed from Monday to Wednesday because of the Blizzard. The undertaker could not pull his horsedrawn hearse through the snow-choked streets. Runners and ropes were attached to the casket and several men pulled it through the streets, first to the dead woman's home where the body was placed in the coffin, and then to the cemetery. Interment was still impossible. More than three feet of snow covered gravemarkers making it difficult to find the family plot.

The death toll continued to mount hourly as more missing persons were discovered frozen in snow banks. The obituary columns were also fattened by out-of-condition shovelers who were felled by heart attacks as they attempted to move tons of snow from sidewalks and roofs. Coroners and health boards were besieged with requests for burial permits.

The gravediggers' vacation came to an abrupt end when cemetery roads were cleared and delayed funerals were rescheduled. More than 130 funerals, some held up as much as five days by the storm, took place at New York's Calvary Cemetery alone on Friday after the Blizzard.

At least one man and two children escaped death by burrowing into the snow and remaining there for hours until the storm subsided. In Waterford, Connecticut, nine-year-old Gordon Chappelle and his four-year-old sister Legrona became lost in the Blizzard as they tried to reach an aunt's house where their mother was tending to a sick relative. The children started out in the late afternoon and took shelter behind a stone wall. The snow quickly covered them. A dozen men tramped through the storm for hours looking for the children, discovering them only after prodding the snow with a heavy cane. Although their hands and ears were frostbitten, both survived. In a similar situation, Joseph Jennings of New Haven, Connecticut, was overcome by the snow while walking home from work on Tuesday afternoon. Using only his hands, he dug a snow cave in the bottom of a deep drift and remained there until 9 a.m. on Wednesday. Jennings suffered no ill effects from the ordeal.

Stories about the discovery of persons trapped and frozen in snow drifts did have a humorous side. While clumping through the storm in Danbury, one unidentified man stumbled on an obstruction buried in the snow and was sent sprawling over what appeared to be a human form. With a yell that could be heard above the roar of the wind, he ran into the nearest saloon informing the patrons that he had found someone frozen in a snow drift. The entire party ran out to exhume the body, only to find that they had rescued a wooden cigar store Indian which had toppled from its perch in the gale.

*Persons wanting to cross the street in Pough-keepsie, New York, had to stoop low to go through this tunnel. (Dutchess County Historical Society)*

*Street cleaning crews shovel the sidewalk on 6th Avenue. During the storm, entrepreneurs raised rickety ladders to stuck trains on the elevated tracks and charged passengers as much as two dollars to come down. (The New York Historical Society)*

*Four girls are dwarfed by massive snow drifts on Hurricane Road in Westmoreland, New Hampshire. (Historical Society of Cheshire County)*

*Young and old contemplate the damage left behind by the Blizzard at the corner of Main and Prospect Streets in Bristol, Connecticut. (Bristol Historical Society)*

## Beating the Elements — Blizzard Fashions

Bizarre clothing resurrected from forgotten trunks in dusty attics helped garb those who had to face the frigid winds and pelting snow. *The New York Times* enjoyed a field day describing the odd outfits improvised during the Blizzard.

> The styles of headdresses in the streets yesterday have not been rivaled in ten years. Caps of bearskin, muskrat fur, and even cat skins were worn. Toboggan caps of fancy colors were very popular, especially when worn with white woolen leggings.

The *New York World* also relished the makeshift fashions of the Blizzard:

> A more fantastic procession you would go far to find. Some wore blankets tied about their heads. Some had their hair protected by vari-colored kerchiefs. Some stalked in huge rubber boots. Others showed part of their wisdom by having their trouser legs tied tightly about the ankle, and not a few, emulating the wise and foxy tramp, bundled their feet in squares of carpeting, and were very happy.

Though city dwellers wore hats of every size and description, many of those headgear ended up as litter on the streets. Those not whisked away by the wind swiftly fell victim to young boys with snowballs. Hundreds of men and women cut holes in handkerchiefs and kerchiefs making masks to guard their faces against the wind's sandblasting effect.

Shovelers digging out drifts often came upon headwear, blown from the pates of hapless storm victims. When Captain John Batchelder's expensive new chapeau was blown clean over the roof of his home in Concord, New Hampshire, a companion asked why he didn't chase it immediately. The veteran replied, "It's in Suncook [a town ten miles away] by this time!"

## Hello, Central!

Invented a decade earlier, the telephone had made an enormous impact on life in 1888. Telephone companies sprang up almost overnight, covering cities with a web of wires strung from poles already overburdened by telegraph and electrical cables.

The fortunes of the telephone operators (or "operatives" as they were referred to in many newspaper accounts) were not happy ones during the hours of the Blizzard. In Worcester, Massachusetts, 15 operators sat before a spaghetti bowl of plugs and wires handling three times the normal volume of calls. Nearly half were directed to Union Station, the only source of quick information about stranded trains. Often, callers were placed in a queue, waiting hours to reach the desired party. One operator rose to the defense of the overworked telephone employees in an interview with a *Worcester Daily Telegram* reporter:

> "In all my experience," said one of the operatives, "I have never had so many calls to answer, nor so many cranks to deal with. Your reporters have a good deal to say concerning sleepy operatives and operative's neglect; but one hour in this exchange this afternoon would convince you that the operatives themselves are the real sufferers."

In Hartford, telephone operators worked nonstop from 7 a.m. until 6 p.m. Managers said there had been nothing like it since service was established ten years earlier. The city's telephone system remained relatively intact during the entire storm, allowing anxious housekeepers to deluge markets and grocers with calls about overdue deliveries. A single telephone line served as Hartford's only communication link with Boston, which let newspaper editors get some meager news coverage from the outside world.

*While housekeepers inundated grocery stores with telephone inquiries about late or missed deliveries, grocers wondered how they would make deliveries through snow-clogged streets. In Keene, New Hampshire, horsedrawn sleds were used to bring orders from Wilbur's Market to customers on the day after the Blizzard. (Historical Society of Cheshire County)*

The young boy at left waves to the photographer while the staff of Archibald McClure & Co. peer out the window in this photograph taken on Main Street in Albany, New York. (Albany Institute of History and Art)

Bundled against the cold, these children marveled at the deep snow on Elk Street in Albany, New York (Albany Institute of History and Art)

## The Threat of Fire

With streets choked by snow and the progress of clearing operations slow, city officials in the Blizzard-paralyzed cities wondered how they would cope with a major fire. Sketchy news reports told of a fire at the storm's height that destroyed much of Stamford, Connecticut. Although the reports proved false — the blaze had been confined to a telegraph office at the Stamford depot — the threat still loomed. A major fire would be catastrophic. Hydrants were buried under snow drifts. Horses pulling fire trucks could not maneuver through the snow-congested streets.

Fire was a primary concern for Albany's mayor John Boyd Thatcher. Recognizing the potential for conflagration and calling upon citizens to perform a civic duty, Thatcher issued an urgent proclamation:

To the citizens of Albany:

The unprecedented storm of snow has rendered our streets impassable, and should a fire break out in the present condition of our thoroughfares, no help could be expected from fire apparatus.

The street commissioner is at work with his full force clearing the streets, especially about the hydrants. I ask our citizens to aid in this immense labor, and as soon as possible, to employ at their own expense men and teams in clearing a passageway in the streets in front of their residences and places of business. Householders and manufacturers are urged to exercise particular caution in guarding against fire.

Yours, John Boyd Thatcher
Mayor of Albany

Thatcher's concern about the potential for disastrous fires was warranted. At the height of the Blizzard most of business area in Clifton Falls, New York, was consumed by a blaze that broke out in a dry goods store. Hazardous chemicals stored by retailers contributed to the disaster; two workers were severely injured when a keg of gunpowder exploded in an adjacent hardware store. Firemen were helpless to stop the blaze.

Municipal fire departments took unusual steps to cope with the potential for conflagrations. In Ansonia, Connecticut, the Eagle Hose and Fountain Hose Companies found streets impassable. Hose from the horsedrawn wagon was uncoupled and tied in lengths that could be carried by a single firefighter. Each man would take a length of hose on his shoulder and run as fast as possible to the fire. By Tuesday, a horsedrawn toboggan sled had been procured and packed with 400 feet of coupled hose ready for service.

Downed telegraph lines crippled fire departments in major cities like New York. By 4 p.m. Monday, almost half of the 1,000 fire alarm boxes in Manhattan were out of order. If a major fire broke out, there was a good chance that no one would be able to call the fire department in some neighborhoods.

*Looking down Fulton Street in Troy, New York. (Rensselaer County Historical Society)*

*Snow is loaded in carts and hauled away in Troy, New York's Franklin Square. The building in the center contained the offices and studios of several photographers, including some who took photographs used in this volume. One — Lloyd's Studio — is still in business 100 years later. (Rensselaer County Historical Society)*

When fire did break out in a West 42nd Street tenement Tuesday afternoon, six horses had a terrible struggle dragging a fire engine over the drifts for the three-block trip from the station. Hope that more equipment could be brought to the scene was abandoned when two other companies arrived on foot with what little gear they could carry. The five-story building was roaring and crackling when the firefighters arrived. Flames already pierced the roof. Lacking equipment, firemen could only concentrate on saving adjacent buildings. While they hindered firemen, the tall snow drifts proved to be lifesavers for a few of the building's residents. When they jumped from upper story windows, their fall was cushioned by the drifts. A total of sixty families, including a woman dying of tuberculosis, was turned out into the Blizzard. Many escaped with only the clothes on their back.

Firefighters in Camden, New Jersey, fretted over a different problem — the low water level in the Delaware River, which threatened the city's water supply. Firemen feared that they would not be able to get enough water pressure from hydrants if a conflagration erupted.

## Getting Home

For those who managed to get to work on Monday morning, returning home at day's end proved to be an even greater nightmare. By the time night fell, all public transportation in areas affected by the storm had ceased. Hack drivers flatly refused to take on passengers, fearing that horses would succumb to the sub-zero wind chill.

Urban streets, normally lit by the warm glow of gas lights, were plunged into darkness. Gas lights were individually lighted by men who patrolled the streets at dusk to turn on the quaint lanterns. Drifts and snow banks put most gas street fixtures out of the lighter's reach. Those few lanterns that were lit quickly blew out in the howling winds. In areas where street lights had been converted to electricity, a few remained on, but most were extinguished when the wind snapped telegraph poles. Darkness and blinding snow made landmarks invisible. Street signs were also impossible to read. For those who waited until nightfall to make the journey home, it was as if they had been plunged into a blackened cave.

# HARPER'S WEEKLY.

## JOURNAL OF CIVILIZATION.

Vol. XXXII.—No. 1631.
Copyright, 1888, by HARPER & BROTHERS.
All Rights Reserved.

NEW YORK, SATURDAY, MARCH 24, 1888.

TEN CENTS A COPY.
WITH A SUPPLEMENT.

A STRUGGLE TO ANSWER A FIRE-ALARM DURING THE NEW YORK BLIZZARD.—Drawn by T. de Thulstrup.

**AFTER THE GREAT STORM, MARCH 13, 1888**

*A tunnel wide enough to drive a team of oxen through was dug on Hardscrabble Road in Chesterfield, New Hampshire. The construction crew etched the date on the arch by pressing stones into the hard-packed snow. (Historical Society of Cheshire County)*

Shamgar Babcock was mechanical manager of the *Sag Harbor Express* newspaper at the time of the Blizzard. In a letter to the Blizzard Men of '88, he recalled being trapped in a second floor office during the storm.

> By night the drift had reached the second story window sill. When we were ready to depart at 6 o'clock we found a solid wall of snow as the lower door was opened. . . . We did have two shovels. It was necessary to tunnel through for about fifteen feet, carrying the snow upstairs and throwing it out the back windows. Making an exit . . . our combined strength weathered the gale in an almost exhausted condition.

A young woman from Putney, Vermont, journeyed to Brattleboro on Monday's early morning train to make some final purchases for her wedding trousseau. By afternoon the drifting snow had obliterated the railroad tracks. Walking the distance home was impossible, so the young woman unwillingly spent the night in Brattleboro. As the snow continued falling on Tuesday, so did the young woman's tears. Her wedding was set for that day, but she had no way to reach her fiance with the news that it was only the snow, and not last-minute doubts about the impending union, that kept her from flying to her beloved's arms.

## The Pub With No Beer

From the corner gin mill to the exclusive private club, liquor-serving establishments did a booming business throughout the storm. In many areas, they were the only havens from the awful wind and snow. Beleaguered pedestrians stayed all day in unfamiliar taverns rather than renew the struggle. Hard liquor was the drink of the day; most establishments ran out of beer before afternoon on the first day of the storm. In the days before refrigeration, beer was a perishable commodity served only from kegs supplied by local breweries. Tap room owners depended on daily deliveries of fresh kegs, keeping only a small supply on hand — a stock that was quickly consumed. With brewery wagons stalled and abandoned, beer soon became a scarce staple.

Pubs benefited from an old wives' tale, too. Drinking alcoholic beverages was viewed by many as a way to fortify oneself against the cold. This illusion of warmth and strength from stiff drink undoubtedly contributed to many deaths and frostbite injuries during the Blizzard. Police officers pulled many victims from drifts in an alcoholic stupor. The *New York Herald* described the situation this way:

> There had been a universal carousal in the saloons all day. Men had filled themselves with whiskey in order to resist the effects of the cold. Drunken men reeled out of the rum shops and staggered into the deep snow. While daylight lasted these men were soon discovered and rescued. But when darkness closed in and the storm raged over a city plunged in utter blackness the police began to realize the frightful responsibility thrown upon them of saving human life. . . . Drunken men and men who were simply tired by long and severe struggles in the drifts were stumbled over in every neighborhood.

Most intoxicated persons picked up by police were taken to holding cells for the night. Even that proved to be a poor sanctuary for some. Found in a snow drift and brought before the judge on a charge of public drunkenness during the Blizzard, Thomas Gleason was sentenced to ten days in New York City's Tombs Prison. Within a day, Gleason was dead from the effects of exposure.

**ONE OF MANY.**

The horses cared for at John L. Ray's Livery Stable in Brattleboro, Vermont, didn't care one bit for the task of pulling sleds and wagons through the deep snow. Many times carts and other horsedrawn vehicles were stalled because the horses would not lift their legs over mounds of snow. (Brattleboro P.H.O.T.O.S.)

GOOD HEAVENS FRIEND HOW CAN YOU WEAR AN OVERCOAT AND LOOK SO COOL
THIS WARM WEATHER?
I ALWAYS BRING MY OVERCOAT DOWN TOWN, AS I FIND AFTER DRINKING A GLASS
OF "BLAKELY'S BLIZZARD SODA," DRAWN FROM HIS "ARCTIC FOUNTAIN," THAT I AM COLD
THE BALANCE OF THE DAY.

## The Entrepreneurial Spirit

Two days before the Blizzard, the owner of the only restaurant in Mount Vernon, New York, filed a bankruptcy petition in the local court. When thousands of stranded rail commuters took refuge in the town's train station, the restaurateur saw a chance for financial salvation. The price of sandwiches suddenly jumped to five dollars each. Hungry travellers eagerly snapped up the only food in town, paying the price to satisfy the gnawing ache in their stomachs. An estimated 6,000 sandwiches were served. Two days after the Blizzard, he tore up the bankruptcy papers. By then he was the richest man in town.

It was an experience repeated over and over in cities and towns affected by the Blizzard as owners of small businesses saw their chance to become a tycoon in a day. The storm brought out some of the worst in human nature, and greed was the motivating factor.

Nearly everyone fortunate enough to possess a tool or other items useful to those stuck in the Blizzard found a way to become an entrepreneur. On New York's Sixth Ave. elevated near 22nd Street, two men set up a ladder against the structure to rescue passengers stuck in cars above. Shuddering in the wind, the ladder barely reached the top of the iron railway structure. Two wooden boxes were placed under the lowest rung to gain a few extra feet of height. With the shaky arrangement in place, the ladder's owner calmly shouted that passengers who wanted to climb down could do so for just 25 cents each. The offer was cheerfully accepted by those who wanted the privilege of coming down to street level to freeze instead of in the cars. When all passengers had alighted, the ladder owners walked away with $100 in quarters. The good fortune of the enterprising ladder owners didn't go unnoticed for long. Soon more neighborhood residents raised ladders to other stalled trains, but by now the ante had been upped. The ladder fare went as high as two dollars.

PIE GOOD ENOUGH FOR THEM.

*Facing page: The Blizzard spawned a number of products including Blakeley's Blizzard Soda. (The New York Historical Society)*

*A tunnel big enough to drive a sleigh through in front of "the sweetest place in town" — the Curtis and Frasier Confectionery Shop in Saratoga Springs, New York. (Collection of George S. Bolster)*

At Wilbur's Market in Keene, New Hampshire, horsedrawn sleds are loaded with groceries and other supplies for delivery to customers immediately after the Blizzard. (Historical Society of Cheshire County)

## A Cause for Celebration

Despite howling winds and treacherous drifts, some persons found the Blizzard a cause to celebrate.

At the Manchester, New Hampshire, home of Mr. and Mrs. H. T. Grace, a crazy tea party chased away the storm's gloom for 20 members of the city's Wide Awake Club. Costume-clad club members sat down to a dinner of beans served in pitchers and bread from dustpans. After the repast, party goers participated in a number of "social amusements," including a pig drawing contest in which everyone present was required to sketch a pig while blindfolded. The entertainments continued past midnight when guests retreated home in the frigid weather warmed by the hospitality of the hosts.

When a large number of rail passengers found themselves stranded in Arlington, New Jersey, town residents opened their homes to strangers. One passenger had brought a fiddle in his baggage and soon had guests and hosts singing and dancing to a lively beat. A dry goods merchant chilled spines with ghost stories, while another businessman led a lively discussion on government regulation of business. When tracks were cleared sufficiently to permit trains to leave, the passengers took lunch baskets generously prepared by Arlington's citizens.

Three trains and four locomotives wait out the storm near the entrance to a tunnel on the New York and Susquehanna Railroad. (Connecticut State Library)

The snow and cancellation of school in many municipalities brought joy to the faces of children. The Blizzard wasn't a disaster, but a winter marvel to a child's imagination. Most parents forbid their children to go outside at the height of the storm, but at least one adolescent girl was entranced enough to brave the tempest and the scolding she knew would result. Putting on her brother's boots, and her own coat, hat and mittens, Julia Pettee stepped out the door of her Lakeville, Connecticut, home:

> It was glorious. The mighty wind whipped and whirled her about, an exhilarating and joyous dance. She felt herself lifted into the cloud of snow, part of the storm itself. How far she went into this elysium of bliss she did not know but dropped to earth as a sobering moment of fear swept over her, and dimly making out the house, she realized she must get back to safety. The glory of the battle with the elements still held its charm as she fought her way back to the door and still tingling with pleasurable excitement the scolding that greeted her fell on deaf ears.

William N. Beebe of Canaan, Connecticut, was 13-years old at the time of the Blizzard:

> . . . there was a drift . . . which was 20 feet high and we kids dug channels all through it and from the center up through the top — and did we have fun pushing each other down through and falling into the soft snow at the bottom! Then we would crawl out of one of the channels and repeat the performance.

*A demure young lady stands at a tunnel sculptured through the drifts at Miss Porter's School in Farmington, Connecticut. The tunnel had six feet of headroom. (The New York Historical Society)*

## Humor in the Snow

Despite the desperate situation, the Blizzard was treated in a light-hearted way by many who lived through it.

In northern New Hampshire, the *White Mountain Republic* offered this tongue-in-cheek look at some of the storm's casualties:

Liarton, N.Y. was buried beneath fifty feet of snow. The citizens have made tunnels along the sidewalks and at the street crossings by eating the snow as they proceed. In the center of the town they have tunnelled out to the surface of the drift. To avoid a disastrous flood about the next 4th of July, the mayor has issued a proclamation requiring each citizen to eat ten cubic feet of snow a day until the streets are cleared.

At Punkerton, VT., the thermometer dropped to 97° below zero. The town is well supplied with fuel, but the fires keep freezing up as fast as people can light them. One hundred of the prominent citizens have already notified the coroner that they are dead.

DRIFT !

## 200 Feet !

DOWN PEARL STREET !

AND VISIT

## RIPLEY BROTHERS,

## New Carpet Store.

EVERYTHING

### In New Decorations.

Special Features in Wall Paper and Drapery Departments.

## No. 49 Pearl Street.

*Puns about snow were quick to appear in newspaper advertisements placed by retailers after the storm. (The Connecticut Historical Society)*

*The king of the mountain? Maybe. The Bridgeport, Connecticut, jokester who stuck a top hat and a pair of boots in this pile of snow probably wanted to poke fun at the city's gentry. The banner stuck in the snow carries the legend "Excelsior." (The Connecticut Historical Society)*

Snow drifts offered many opportunities for practical jokers and wags. In several cities, pranksters upended a pair of old boots and stuck them on top of a deep drift with a sign indicating the final resting place of some prominent citizen. By Thursday, merchants had placarded drifts close to their doors with advertisements offering free samples or sacrifice prices on snow, or offers such as 1,000 pounds of free snow with every $1 purchase. On New York's City's Broadway, one sign anticipated the racy headlines of the entertainment newspaper *Variety* with "THIS BLIZ KNOCKS BIZ."

In front of one Newark business, an unusual help-wanted advertisement was posted: "500 GIRLS WANTED." Underneath in fine print read the catch: "To Eat Snow." A warning to taletellers appeared in a drift outside a Newark saloon: "Any man who relates any snow reminiscences here will be compelled to treat the house." The conversation among the patrons probably strayed little from politics, the recent prizefight that had captured the heavyweight title for John L. Sullivan and women.

*Merchants, to entertain themselves because of the absence of customers, placarded snow banks with impromptu advertising. This collection of signs blossomed on Hartford's Main Street. Henry Hobson Richardson's castle-like brownstone building housing the Brown Thomson & Co. department store is visible at left. (The Connecticut Historical Society)*

*Two homesteaders stake their claim on a pile of snow in downtown Hartford. The sign reads: "No trespassing on this island." (The Connecticut Historical Society)*

75

John Whitaker Watson's "Beautiful Snow," a poem that appears to have been required memorization by every schoolchild in the late 19th century, was particularly vilified. When a member of a stranded group of rail passengers in New Jersey offered to recite the poem to entertain stranded companions, a collection was taken up to buy him off. The *New Canaan (Connecticut) Messenger* offered "a reward of five cents, good and lawful United States money, for the arrest and conviction of the person who wrote 'Beautiful Snow.'" In Hartford, Connecticut, citizens took the matter into their own hands. A group of vigilantes hung the offending poet in effigy outside the United States Hotel. Dangling over the sidewalk and clad in "dude clothing," red whiskers and a white plug hat, the dummy made an excellent target for young boys with snowballs.

*A reward for the conviction of John Whitaker Watson, author of the poem "Beautiful Snow," was offered by one Fairfield County, Connecticut, newspaper. This version of the poem was found in an album of Hartford Blizzard photographs. (The Connecticut Historical Society)*

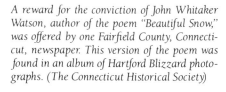

*The author of the poem "Beautiful Snow" hangs in effigy over the sidewalk outside the United States Hotel in downtown Hartford. The mannequin quickly became the target of many snowballs. (The Connecticut Historical Society)*

# Chapter 5 — Stuck! Trying to Get Around In The Blizzard

"Think the train'll get here tonight?"

Thousands of times, station masters and other railroad employees answered this question asked by anxious passengers and those awaiting the arrival of loved ones during the Blizzard of '88 with a terse "I don't know."

For a week in March 1888, the Blizzard brought all rail transportation in the northeast to a standstill. The storm buried trains from Baltimore to Montreal, marooning passengers for as long as seven days. Blocked tracks caused an enormous hiatus as well in the distribution of freight.

No accurate data exist on how many trains were stalled by the storm or how many passengers found themselves stranded in cars on the tracks. But thousands of people in fact were stranded, mostly under perilous conditions. As engines became mired in snow drifts, passengers resigned themselves to lengthy stays in cramped and often crowded quarters. Usually there was little or no food. Lucky ones were reached by farmers who came on foot through the drifts with baskets of provisions for halted trains. On a few routes railroad employees shared the contents of their lunch pails, a meager ration at best. Freezing temperatures reigned in drafty cars. The small coal or wood stoves offered little easement from the cold. When fuel ran out, card tables and seats were chopped up and stuffed in heaters to provide momentary relief from the unbearable cold. Many left the trains on foot on a dangerous search for food, warmth and shelter.

Railroad traffic controllers typically used the telegraph to inform stations up the line that a train had passed. Downed wires knocked out almost all communication between stations, giving no clues as to the whereabouts of trains. Without accurate knowledge of the progress of trains or if they were snowbound, railroad officials could do nothing to relieve the suffering of passengers aboard stalled cars or reach them with food, fuel or other survival supplies.

*Planting a shovel atop a pile of snow removed from a sidewalk, one Manhattanite heads for the grocer to fill up a coal bucket to provide some warmth in chilly rooms during the Blizzard. (Connecticut State Library)*

In station waiting rooms the crowds gathered. Freight depots filled up with trunks, packages and sundry baggage awaiting the arrival of overdue trains. Tempers soon flared. Shouting matches erupted between frustrated patrons and harried railroad employees. One shipper in Manchester, New Hampshire, fumed over 48 barrels of onions and a similar quantity of potatoes on board a stalled freight car that were almost certainly ruined by frost. Disgusted, he retreated to the telegraph office and demanded to know who would pay for the loss.

When a train did manage to struggle into a station, people celebrated. As if aware of the historical significance of the event, railroad employees and passengers would crowd around a snow-covered engine for a group photograph. Hours late, a train from Lawrence, Massachusetts, labored into the Manchester, New Hampshire, depot on the first night of the storm. A reporter described the arrival of the all-white ghost train:

There were only two cars . . . drawn by one lonely looking locomotive. Reaching from the tip end of the cowcatcher and looming up to the headlight was a huge bank of snow almost three feet thick. It looked as though it had picked up a drift somewhere and hated to part with it. Every part of the running machinery was enveloped with a blanket of snow, not a particle of the usually bright and well-cleaned steel work being visible. The locomotive looked as though it was made from snow and just from the ice-king's domains. The cloth curtains of the cab were drawn closely . . . and long fingers of ice showed themselves. When the train came to a standstill, a fireman . . . gazed at the crowd at the depot as though he never expected to see civilization again.

*Shovelers work to clear the tracks while a New York, New Haven & Hartford locomotive waits to pass through a cut in South Norwalk, Connecticut. (Darien Historical Society)*

The prospect of rescuing stranded passengers and restoring lost services did not overjoy railroad officials. "There isn't any road — it has disappeared," snapped Chauncy Depew, president of the New York Central and Hudson River Railroad, to a *New York Times* reporter on the second day of the storm. "There are 18 trains between here [Grand Central Station] and Yonkers and there is no way of getting them down as yet. I understand that all but one were reached with food and other refreshments and the passengers have been made as comfortable as possible. We have 500 to 600 [men] at work clearing out the tunnel. There are cuts solidly packed with snow, 22 feet deep in places. The engines are absolutely snowed under."

The first train to leave Bridgeport, Connecticut, on Monday morning departed the depot at 5:41 a.m. Less than an hour later it was trapped in a drift two miles from the station. The next train was unable to move past the freight yards adjacent to the station. Two trains heading into Bridgeport stalled atop a bridge, and railway officials feared that high winds might blow the engine and cars off the tracks to the Housatonic River below. Most passengers deserted the cars to walk to the station in howling winds and blinding snow, but a few remained behind demanding that the railroad company provide food during the wait.

*Another view of the locomotives in tandem that pulled into the depot at Meriden, Connecticut, after bucking the drifts. (Meriden Historical Society)*

*In the railroad yards behind Grand Central Station, a crew loads snow into coal cars for disposal. (The New York Historical Society)*

More than 1,000 stranded passengers took refuge in the Bridgeport depot, but the storm-enforced layover was made more bearable by some unexpected entertainment. Huddled among the shivering throng were the members of a traveling theater group, who decided to treat the crowd to a stage adaptation of Harriet Beecher Stowe's "Uncle Tom's Cabin," which had been scheduled Monday night at Bridgeport's Hawes Opera House.

To keep passenger service running, the Boston and Albany Railroad cancelled all freight trains at the start of the storm and instead used those engines to double up the locomotive power on its passenger trains, but by mid-afternoon on Monday all trains operated by the company were hopelessly stuck. A switching engine sent out from the Worcester freight yards to retrieve a stalled train got bogged down itself a quarter-mile from the yards.

Where tracks were not blocked by snow drifts, accidents caused by poor visibility often obstructed the right of way. Near Poughkeepsie, New York, a southbound express on the New York Central slammed into the rear of another express inching along in the blinding snow. Traffic in both directions along the main line route was backed up by the wreckage.

## The Big City Besieged

The Blizzard of '88 shut down New York City's transportation system, the first time in its history the city had been completely paralyzed. Loaded wagons ground to a halt first, then the horse cars, and finally the steam-powered elevated railways succumbed to the relentless snow. Yet workers were undaunted in their desperate push to reach their jobs by any means possible. Those lucky enough to board an operating horse car or elevated train often found themselves stranded, abandoned by drivers who thought they could go no further or, worse, stuck high above the streets in an elevated car with a hazardous descent down a shaky wind-whipped ladder the only route to safety.

One elevated train engineer was killed and more than 20 persons injured in an accident at the height of Monday's morning rush hour on the Third Ave. elevated line. A train heading downtown with more than 500 passengers aboard came to a stop when ice-coated rails made it impossible to climb an upgrade just beyond the 76th Street station. After standing still for 20 minutes, passengers heard a shrill whistle behind them as a second downtown train entered the station. The slippery conditions had the opposite effect this time — the second engine could not stop. Air brakes were useless as the second train slid along the rails like a runaway sleigh. Seeing the impending collision, the second engine's fireman hurled himself to the platform as the train passed, screaming "Jump, for God's sake, jump" to the engineer on the stricken train. To the horror of hundreds waiting and watching on the platform, the runaway train rammed into the stalled cars with a thunderous crash just 100 feet down the line. The second engine telescoped into the rearmost passenger car, and a cloud of steam from the damaged engine obscured the view. The trains shuddered perilously for a moment, but by some miracle, all of the cars stayed on the track avoiding the additional loss of life and injuries that would have occurred had they plunged to the streets below.

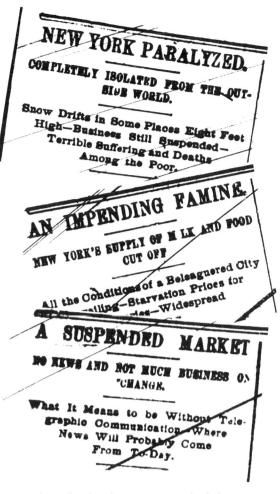

Elevated railroad car passengers climb down a wind-shaken ladder to escape from a train stranded between stations. (Connecticut State Library)

81

*Two men attempt to dig out derailed street-cars abandoned on a Manhattan street while winds whip broken wires above their heads. (Connecticut State Library)*

Passengers on the wrecked trains panicked. Women screamed and men scrambled to find exits from the damaged cars. Every window in the passenger compartments was smashed by people trying to escape. Astonishingly, there was only a single fatality, Samuel Towle, engineer of the second train. Pulled alive from the wreckage, he died minutes later, his body horribly mangled and burned by steam and coals from the firebox. Injured passengers were carried along the tracks back to the 76th Street station where a makeshift hospital was set up on the station platform. Firemen raised ladders to the sides of the platform to retrieve passengers stranded in the wrecked cars.

Users of street-level transportation fared no better than their counterparts riding the rails above the streets. Horses unable to lift their legs above the level of drifting snow balked and refused to pull the load of a street car filled with passengers. Derailments were common. Drivers fearing for their own safety or that of the draft horses simply abandoned both cars and passengers when the going got too tough. Grumbling, passengers were forced to trust their fate to the streets and continue to their destinations on foot.

Walter Hall was a driver on the street cars that ran from 99th Street down to the Bowery.

When I reported for work on Tuesday morning the boss said, "Take the horses and go down as far as you can." Half the time I was on the tracks and half the time I was over the curb. I stuck it out till I got down to the Bowery. There I stopped my poor horses . . . and I said to the passengers, "This is as far as the car goes!"

I gathered up some coal in the neighborhood and filled up the boxes underneath the seats so I'd have plenty to stoke the little stove. And there I stayed from Tuesday to Friday. First night out, after I'd stretched out on the seat, came a banging on the door. Two fellers said, "Can we come in?" I saw they had a keg of beer with them. I was guarding my car all right and I said, "You can come in if you behave yourselves." They said they had a load of beer out there they had to guard, so they'd behave. So there we three stayed Tuesday to Friday, living on beer and pretzels.

*Students cavort in the snow on the campus of Yale University. (New Haven Colony Historical Society)*

Horsedrawn cabs, the favored method of transportation for well-to-do Manhattanites, managed no better in the snow-choked streets. Police could do little to enforce regulations relating to fares, and hack drivers charged what the traffic would bear. As the morning rush hour started on Monday, drivers charged a minimum of ten dollars per passenger. But prices increased exponentially as the snow piled deeped on the streets. Brokers compelled to go downtown to the financial district in order to meet contracts paid extortionate sums for transportation. Naturally, the fare was cash in advance.

*Railroad ties are used to prop up a derailed engine that left the tracks while clearing snow in Fairfield, Connecticut. (Fairfield County Historical Society)*

*Even on a clear day the sidewalks of the Brooklyn Bridge are buffeted by high winds. Police did what they could to deter crossings on foot when the snow flew, but some foolhardy individuals tried the journey anyway. The wait for the five-cent cable car was agonizingly long owing to equipment breakdowns. (The Library of Congress)*

The *New York Herald* reported on one such transaction between a broker anxious to consummate a $30,000 deal and an Irish hack driver:

> "I must get down," he [the broker] pleaded.
>
> "Ah, very loikly," said the driver, sticking his tongue in cheek and breaking a few icicles from his beard.
>
> "What will you take for your whole establishment?"
>
> "It aren't moine."
>
> "I'll buy the horse and cab and I'll buy you, too, if you're for sale. Come, what is your price?"
>
> "The 'orse arn't moine, oi tell ye."
>
> "Your rig is worth $150. Come, I'll give you $300."
>
> "No, but oi'll take ye down for $50."
>
> The broker paid it.

Manhattan's geographical situation compounded the frustration of those who wanted to get into the city or get out. No bridges crossed the Hudson River in 1888. All commuter railroads serving New Jersey communities terminated at one of several ferry terminals for the connecting boat ride to Manhattan. A northeast gale hurled heavy seas against the ferry slips and made the short journey across the river perilous. Crossings that normally took five or ten minutes stretched to hours. Overloaded with passengers, the ferries had great difficulty finding their way in the driving storm. Visibility in the thick, blowing snow was nil, and captains were hard pressed to find the usual berths on the opposite shore. After the storm, one ferry captain was heard to say that his greatest fear was that one false move would overturn his boat.

The few ferries that continued running soon had to contend with another problem. When a ferry carrying 25 passengers from Jersey City approached its Cortland Street berth after a 45-minute journey across the Hudson, it found the slip was completely filled with ice. With no place to land, the captain headed back to the Jersey shore only to find that ice had clogged the Jersey City dock, too. The boat drifted to a nearby commercial pier, one of the few still ice-free. Soon the ice surrounded that berth as well, preventing the ferry from leaving. Passengers made the best of the situation; a jug of "Jersey lightning" and an all-night poker game helped pass the time.

Getting from Manhattan back to Brooklyn was just as difficult, even though the Brooklyn Bridge had spanned the East River for five years. East River ferries still carried much of the passenger traffic between the two cities. (Brooklyn would not become one of the five boroughs of New York City until several years later.) Police closed the bridge to pedestrian and wagon traffic early on Monday, fearing that the violent winds would blow someone over the railing into the frigid waters below. Cable cars traversing the Brooklyn Bridge made unsteady progress in the Blizzard. A three-car train jumped the tracks near the Manhattan terminus blocking the tracks completely for about two hours Monday morning. By 3 p.m. the platform and waiting room on the Manhattan side were packed with impatient passengers, and many of those anxious to get home were forced to stand outside in the snow. A riot almost broke out when angry passengers broke through a wooden barricade near the ticket takers. Hundreds stampeded up the stairs and jammed their bodies in among the hundreds already waiting on the platform. Police were powerless to control the vociferous crowd.

The situation changed little on Tuesday morning. Although no horsecars were running in Brooklyn, the elevated trains managed to bring a substantial number of passengers to the cable car terminus. By 8 a.m. the streets outside the ticket windows on the Brooklyn side of the bridge were filled with a pushing and struggling crowd attempting to get to jobs in Manhattan. The cable mechanism had frozen solid as temperatures plunged overnight. Only a single train pulled by a small steam engine was running on the bridge, hardly enough to handle the passenger demand. Some tried walking across the bridge. Most just grumbled about the situation.

A capsized vessel lies on its side in the shallow waters of Lewes Harbor. Behind it, the broken masts of a schooner point skyward at odd angles. (Delaware State Archives)

Shovelers work to clear railroad tracks that ran down the middle of one of Newark, New Jersey's main streets. (The New Jersey Historical Society)

SUBURBAN TRAINS SNOWBOUND.

Before sunrise, a huge field of ice covering hundreds of acres floated down the East River past Manhattan toward the Battery. Wider than the river, the enormous ice floe twisted dock pilings out of shape as it struck and got stuck just south of the Brooklyn Bridge.

The ice blocked the Fulton Street ferry to the consternation of Brooklyn commuters who gathered for their morning journey to Manhattan. The hundreds who thronged at the gateway grew impatient. One daring spirit jumped from the dock to the ice. Testing it with a few hesitating steps, he soon confidently strode across the floe toward the city. His progress was anxiously noted by others waiting on the dock, but when it appeared that the route was secure, others followed. Within 15 minutes, a struggling line of pedestrians stretched across the river.

Fishmongers and longshoremen near the ferry terminal, whose livelihood had been temporarily cut off by the weather, soon found an alternate source of income. Ladders were brought to the edge of the docks, and eager commuters were charged a nickel for the descent to the ice. By 9 a.m., a tug had cleared the ice on Fulton Street ferry slip and the boats resumed their journey, but that still didn't deter hundreds more persons who crossed the river on the ice. The crossing was a reckless adventure; most did it just for the bragging rights. Estimates of how many persons made the crossing varied, but at least several thousand walked across the ice bridge.

High tide arrived at 9:46 a.m. Pedestrians disregarded the warnings of longshoreman who knew that the outgoing tide would soon have a destructive effect on the ice bridge. Even though ladders were pulled up, many foolhardy walkers insisted on starting the trek. About 10 a.m., the ice began to loosen from its moorings. A hundred or more persons were still on the floe and many began to run toward the closest shore point. Several minutes later, with a creak and groan that could be heard from end to end, the entire floe began to move seaward.

*A few of the hardy (some say foolhardy) souls who crossed the East River on a temporary ice bridge that formed on the morning of March 13. (Museum of the City of New York)*

As it flowed past the Black Ball dock, about 40 people crowded to the edge of the ice but were unable to reach the pier. The ice continued to move toward the harbor, tantalizingly close to the docks on the Manhattan side, but just out of reach. Some laughed in the excitement; others sank to their knees and prayed. The floe grated against the Mallory pier and stayed motionless for five minutes, enough time to lower ladders and get off those gathered on the edge.

A few frightened souls who had attempted to cross from Manhattan to Brooklyn were still on the ice as it loosened its tenuous grip for the last time. A tug began to break up the ice mass, slicing the floe like pie crust to prevent damage to ships in the harbor. Three terrorized men who had begun the crossing together suddenly found themselves stranded on three separate parts of the floe. Shouting frantically with arms flapping, they tried to hail other tugs for a rescue. One man ran frantically on his cake of ice causing the edges to dip in the frigid waters below. All three drifted near a dock where onlookers threw ropes to the stranded men. The distance was only about 50 feet, but the wind spoiled the aim of the would-be rescuers. Finally, a tug maneuvered close enough to get a line to each man and haul him aboard. A fourth stranded individual got within 50 feet of the Brooklyn shore, jumped into the nippy waters and was pulled up on the docks.

*Frustrated commuters try their luck at crossing the Brooklyn Bridge on foot. The Brooklyn Bridge cable cars that normally carried thousands of passengers each day broke down and could only provide limited service during the Blizzard. (The New York Historical Society)*

## On City Streets

Outside New York City, horse car companies in municipalities from New Jersey to New Hampshire found the going on city streets tough. The relentless fury of the storm closed routes off as fast as pathways could be opened.

Street railways in Bridgeport tried removing snow with plows pulled by teams of 10 horses. After the first few hours of the snowfall when huge drifts made the streets totally impassable, these efforts were abandoned.

The *Morning News* in Danbury, Connecticut, lauded the local street railway's attempts to keep the tracks clear by sending out a sweeper and scraper at 2 a.m., shortly after snow began to accumulate. This effort was also doomed, as drifting snow quickly filled in the streets again.

Heroic efforts to keep horse car tracks open in Hartford also proved fruitless as the winds piled drifts across stretches of track immediately after they were cleared. Although cars were sent out on time on Monday morning, round trips that normally took 20 minutes stretched to two hours or more in the blinding snow. By mid-afternoon, tracks were hopelessly blocked and all cars were recalled to the car barns.

As soon as the snowfall abated, plows drawn by teams of eight horses attempted to clear streetcar tracks. Rushing at obstinate snow drifts higher than the horses' heads, drivers often had to extricate the animals buried in the snow. By Friday when the tracks were opened enough to insure some semblance of a normal schedule, the Hartford Horse Railroad estimated that close to $10,000 had been spent to remove the snow.

*Employees of the Pacific Iron Works and Miller Lumber Company pose around an abandoned horsecar on Bridgeport's Housatonic Avenue. (Bridgeport Public Library)*

Horsedrawn street cars in Worcester, Massachusetts, began their Monday morning runs taking men and women to mills, factories and stores. For the first few moments of the morning rush hour all went well, but the snow collected rapidly. Drivers began doubling up teams, using four horses to pull a car instead of the usual two. As the air turned almost opaque with snow, the jaded horses puffed and steamed, struggling to pull wheels that had become hopelessly clogged and refused to rotate. The cars were dragged deadweight like sleighs, slipping over snow that buried the iron rails. Passengers were often asked to push the cars from the rear while horses strained in their harnesses to pull in front. Commuters in nearby Fitchburg also fared poorly. The two-and-a-half feet of snow and drifts ranging from ten to twenty feet high stalled horse car traffic from the evening of the 12th until the afternoon of the 23rd.

*Six horses pull the first plow to break through the drifts on Hartford's Main Street. (The Connecticut Historical Society)*

*Snow removed from Hartford's streets was dumped off wagons at the end of Trumbull Street, near the site of Bushnell Park. (The Connecticut Historical Society)*

A horsecar driver in Manchester, New Hampshire, during the height of the Blizzard resembled "one of the 'tall and sheeted ghosts' of Whittier's 'Snow Bound,' " according to an eyewitness who told his story in the local newspaper. A hat pulled low and a tightly wound scarf exposed only a few square inches of the driver's face, but that flesh bared to the wind was the color of raw beef. His prodigious mustache drooped from the weight of miniature icicles hanging on each end. When asked how he felt about being on duty during the Blizzard, the driver answered bitterly:

> Well, sir, if I was a blasted iceberg, I suppose I should rejoice; but as I happen to be nothing but a man, I think it's rough. How would you like it? It's curious to see how the old storm cuts round a feller's head, and how many whacks she gets at him when he least expects it. You fellers, who just get a smell of it riding, don't know nothing about it. You stand outside for two minutes and then you dodge inside. This has been a lonely berth for me today.

Nashua, New Hampshire's horse car company had a novel solution for serving its passengers. Instead of trying to clear the rails with plows, they removed the benches from the horse cars and nailed them to horsedrawn flatbed sleds. This arrangement allowed the company to resume its regular schedule almost without interruption as soon as the snow stopped falling.

*A four-horse team pulling a heavy sled packs down the snow on Keene, New Hampshire's streets. (Keene Public Library)*

# Fighting the Snow

Persons who lived near railroad right of ways were frequently treated to a spectacle that many had never seen before as steam locomotives blasted their way through snowdrifts. A reporter for *The Evening News* in Danbury described it this way:

> In many places the drifts were from ten to twenty-five feet high. After clearing a space through the lighter snow for some distance, the engines, in general two or three in number, would run back as far as possible, and then crowding on all steam, the engineer would send the great mass of iron toward the equally ponderous mass of snow, at a rate of forty to fifty miles an hour. As the engine would dash by it looked as if it must tunnel directly through the snow.

> The cow catcher strikes the drift, sending showers of pieces fifty feet in the air, and going a little farther the drift splits upward, and the smoke stack of the locomotive is seen emerging from the white mass. It makes one or two spasmodic efforts to go forward, but the drivers slipping on the rails refuse to budge an inch. Then the lever is reversed, but still the monster cannot be stirred. Another locomotive is coupled on behind, and an attempt is made to draw out the first, but generally with no better success.

> It is now that a small army of laborers is called on, and after perhaps ten minutes, but more frequently after hours of digging, the engine is released. After taking a short rest, work is again commenced and the operation is repeated. Finally the drift is cleared, and with a shout, the gang moves on to the next.

> Inside the forward locomotive the scene is altogether different. The engineer stands firmly braced with his hand constantly on the throttle. As they dash forward, the car can be felt to shake from side to side, so great is the speed. As the engine strikes the drift, the force of the shock is sufficient to throw one from his feet. Not a thing can be seen ahead or on the sides but snow, and as the shower rattles down on the roof and the tender, it seems as if the entire machine would be buried. Not a few times the locomotives were completely hidden from sight and those on them were obliged to tunnel out to avoid suffocation.

*A single horse pulls an open sleigh through a mammoth drift in Chesterfield, New Hampshire. (Keene Public Library)*

*Blasting through the snow, a New York, New Haven & Hartford locomotive clears the right of way in Fairfield, Connecticut. (Fairfield County Historical Society)*

Dotthof

An artist for the Daily Graphic depicted the effort to open the railroad between Jersey City and Newark on the Pennsylvania Railroad. (The New York Historical Society)

Facing page: This Sussex Railroad passenger train, making a run from Newton to Waterloo, New Jersey, was derailed by a snow drift near Andover on March 12. It took two days for a rescue train to reach the site of the wreck. The rescue train itself was stuck for a day. (The New Jersey Historical Society)

The hard-packed masses of snow hurtled through the air like cannon-balls as engines drove into track-blocking drifts, often causing damage to trackside structures. In Ossining, New York, four locomotives smashed their way through a drift burying tracks that ran next to the wall of Sing Sing Prison, hurling chunks of ice and snow with enough force to break windows in the guard house at the top of the wall more than 50 feet above the tracks.

The West Shore Railroad, which served New Jersey towns, was the only railroad company in the Blizzard area that had adopted new snow-clearing technology using rotary plows. Even this effort was not enough to keep up with the rapid snowfall that buried the tracks as fast as they could be cleared. Pushed by two or three locomotives, the rotary plows had become standard equipment for railroads serving the midwest and western states. A massive fan chewed the snow in front of the train and blew it to the side through a chute at the top of the fan. Brushes and scrapers under the car cleared the remaining snow.

Track-clearing efforts were not without their dangers. The mass of a deep snow drift often equalled or exceeded that of the steam engines trying to push it out of the way. The highest drifts were often found in the narrow cuts blasted through rock to keep the railroad right of way as level as possible. Often these cuts were just wide enough to admit a locomotive and cars with little leeway on either side. Hemmed in by rock walls, the plows could send the snow in only one direction — up!

On the Friday following the Blizzard, a team of five engines with a snow plow attempted to clear the tracks of the New York and Harlem Railroad near Sharon, New York. The most challenging part of the effort proved to be a cut through solid rock some 30 feet deep, 150 feet long, and filled almost to the top with snow. A slight thaw the previous day followed by freezing temperatures at night had made the packed snow almost as hard as granite.

The five coupled engines charged headlong into the cut at speeds up to forty miles per hour. The first engine penetrated the frozen mass and was immediately buried. Engineers driving the other coupled engines were unable to brake their locomotives, and each telescoped into the engine in front of it. Engineer George Fowler at the throttle of the front engine was killed instantly. Three other crew members died at the scene and five more were critically injured. The rescue effort was compounded by the depth of snow, which made retrieval of the victims all the more difficult. A reporter who visited the scene noted that "nothing [of the front engine] was left sound but the wheels. All parts of it were crushed, twisted and bent beyond any possibility of future use. The other engines were damaged beyond all recognition as locomotives."

The Pennsylvania Railroad tried clearing tracks near its Jersey City yards by coupling together a half-dozen giant steam locomotives. Less than a half mile from their starting point progress became impossible. The six locomotives then reversed direction in an attempt to gain enough headway to crash through the stubborn snow barrier that blocked the tracks. As the locomotives in front reversed throttle, the rearmost engine was jolted by the unanticipated force, jumped the tracks, snapped telegraph poles, leaped over a sidewalk, and crashed into a trackside saloon. Miraculously, the engineer was thrown from the cab and escaped serious injury when a snow drift pillowed his fall. Other crew members fared more poorly, however, suffering broken legs, fractured skulls and multiple injuries. A nearby pawnbroker's shop became an impromptu hospital for the injured. No mention of what happened to the saloon patrons when the engine came crashing through is made in newspaper accounts of the incident.

*Coal cars carried snow removed from the tracks of the New York, New Haven and Hartford Railroad to areas where it could be disposed. Here a snow train pauses at New Haven's Union Station on March 22, 1888. (New Haven Colony Historical Society)*

Usually the engineer or fireman in the front locomotive was injured when a team of engines would slam into a snow bank, but not always. In the early morning hours just after the snow stopped near Henniker, New Hampshire, Charles Smart was part of a 25-man track-clearing crew on the Monadnock Railroad. As three engines working in tandem plowed the snow through a narrow right of way in the mountains, Smart stood on the rear of a platform car just behind the third locomotive. Suddenly snow cascaded up over the train and fell back on the tracks. Swept off the platform by the avalanche, the unlucky crewman was buried in several feet of heavy snow. More than 15 minutes elapsed before Smart could be dug out. Too late. He had suffocated.

Even after tracks were cleaned, accidents and unforeseen circumstances combined to snarl the rails. Near Jersey City, blowing snow filled several hundred feet of a railroad tunnel. As the last shovelfuls were cleared, a boulder embedded in the tunnel's roof came loose and fell onto the tracks, blocking the right of way for an additional day. New York-bound passengers had to disembark inside the tunnel, trudge up a snow-covered hill, and walk a mile to the ferry docks for the trip across the Hudson River to Manhattan.

*Trackworkers dig deep to uncover below grade tracks on the New York, New Haven and Hartford Railroad at South Norwalk, Connecticut. (The New York Historical Society)*

*Drifting snow blocks the entrance to the railroad tunnel leading to Grand Central Station near 90th Street. At right, two locomotives try to blast through the impacted snow. (Connecticut State Library)*

*Anxious passengers wait for the next train at Meriden, Connecticut's depot. (Meriden Historical Society)*

## Stranded in the Club Car

Despite their predicament, stranded passengers on trains maintained an air of Victorian civility and decorum through the long wait for food and rescuers. There was very little else they could do. Men kept indelicate language to a minimum. Card games, gambling, drinking and other forms of raucous entertainment were confined mostly to club cars. For most passengers, time crawled. Boredom became a common foe. Politicians, used to the long hours of ennui associated with their profession, were prepared, though. Stuck between Syracuse and Albany, one group of New York state legislators pulled out a deck of cards and launched into a marathon poker game. On a stalled train near New Haven, a traveling performing group also passed the time playing poker, using jelly beans for chips. Higher and higher stakes became common as the game progressed. The players ate the candy representing the lower value chips.

More than a day went by before help arrived for passengers stranded on a Housatonic Railway train hung up in a drift near Brookfield, Connecticut. A relief train bearing supplies for the marooned passengers was already mired in another drift, and it was up to the Brookfield stationmaster to reach the foundering train on foot. Gathering up a gallon of brandy and all the eggs and bread he could muster from a nearby farm house, the stationmaster struggled along the railroad right of way for several hours before reaching the train. He found the passengers half famished and covered with soot, the result of burning bituminous coal meant for the engine in the small stove used to warm the passenger compartment. Without food for more than 30 hours, each passenger was rationed to one egg and two slices of bread, scanty fare to keep one going for another 24 hours. When the Blizzard subsided on Wednesday, the passengers emerged from the car to labor on foot to the nearest station. Several men and women fainted from exhaustion and had to be carried through the drifts by stronger members of the party.

Passengers marooned on a Newark-bound train operated by the Pennsylvania Railroad decided that it was less risky to attempt a mile and a quarter walk to the station than stay aboard the train without food or fuel for the coal heater stove. One by one, the passengers jumped from the rear platform only to be buried up to their armpits in drifted snow. With the wind at their backs, the group started out on the painful and exhausting journey on foot to Newark's station. At some length, after arriving at the sanctuary of the station, several passengers discovered that their unprotected ears had frozen solid.

Not every railroad traveler suffered during the Blizzard of '88, however. A reporter for the *New York World* trudged up the tracks of the Harlem and New Haven Railroad on snowshoes Tuesday morning and found the passengers on a train stuck near the Fordham station calm.

There is nothing startling in the spectacle of an old lady knitting at the window — not at all. But imagine the old lady calmly knitting at the window of a train half buried in snow . . . knitting as peacefully as though at her own fireside. . . . This was the Harlem train which left Pawling [N.Y.] at 6:10 Monday morning, and this was as far as it had journeyed. The conductor was asleep in the first car, and so Brakeman Henry acted as host to the visitor. He invited him in with princely cordiality, and offered him sandwiches and other tempting viands.

*Elbridge S. Jennings of Wilton (third from left) is congratulated on bringing the first New York, New Haven & Hartford train into the South Norwalk, Connecticut, station after the Blizzard on March 15, 1888. (Wilton Historical Society)*

The calm aboard a Boston and Albany express train stuck several miles outside Springfield, Massachusetts, was broken by an unexpected event that raised the passenger count by one. During the train's 48-hour isolation, a passenger gave birth to a boy. The mother and son suffered no apparent complications because of the ordeal.

Clearing main lines was the first priority. Side tracks and connecting routes had to wait, and so did passenger trains that had the misfortune to be stranded there. Getting the trains out of such predicaments often fell upon the volunteer efforts of local citizens. In Westboro, Massachusetts, Bert Cummings and five other volunteers joined a nighttime relief party to bring food to 50 passengers on a local train stuck in a deep cut. Carrying a pail of coffee and a basket of sandwiches, the party stepped over drifts six to eight feet deep. In some places, the snow was hard packed enough to walk on, while an instant later, a rescuer would sink from sight into a drift. Arriving at the train in darkness, the rescue party found hard packed snow and ice sloped up to the windows of the snowbound train. No steps had to be climbed to enter the car. The drifted snow provided a secure ramp. Inside, the passengers eagerly greeted the rescuers and their cargo. When one passenger noted a cigar in the pocket of a volunteer, a furious bidding war broke out as passengers sought to obtain it.

*Railroad workers attempt to get an engine unstuck from a snowbound rock cut in Bristol, Connecticut. (Bristol Historical Society)*

*Pushing a wicker baby carriage, a young woman does her shopping along Main Street in downtown Springfield, Massachusetts, just after the Blizzard. (Springfield Public Library)*

Hunger often led passengers to investigate the contents of baggage cars for the possibility of food. Stuck between New Haven and Derby, Connecticut, riders aboard one train found 600 pies in the baggage car along with five gallons of oysters and 300 pounds of bacon and pork sausage. Water from melted snow washed the repast down. Another train carrying an opera company bound for Fitchburg, Massachusetts, ended its journey in a drift near Shelburne Falls, Vermont, and was soon buried from sight. Famished passengers broke into the sealed express car to discover a cargo of "Chicago Tenderloins" — rolled beef bound for a Boston grocer. Passengers improvised frying pans from coal shovels, and cooked the steaks by holding them over the passenger car heaters.

Worcester's Union Station offered a picturesque scene as 150 stranded travelers turned the waiting room into a small campsite. Children, sleeping on wooden benches or on the floor, improvised pillows from their parents' coats. The restaurant stayed open until running out of food at about 3 a.m. on Tuesday.

*Two locomotives push a tender to clear the snow on the Naugatuck Railroad in Naugatuck, Connecticut. (Fairfield County Historical Society)*

## Disaster at Lewes Harbor

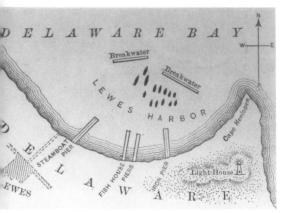

The snug harbor of Lewes, Delaware, provided little refuge for the vessels anchored there during the Blizzard of '88. Wrecks driven aground or smashed to pieces on the stone breakwater and piers littered the area when the winds finally subsided. (Connecticut State Library)

Gale force winds associated with the Blizzard raised havoc along the eastern seaboard. From Cape Hattaras to Portsmouth, New Hampshire, the weather was meaner than many sailors had ever recalled. The harbor of Lewes, Delaware, about 50 miles south of Philadelphia at the mouth of the Delaware River, was hardest hit. Twenty-five vessels were tossed about like toy boats — some up on shore, others on their sides half immersed in frigid ocean waters — all unable to budge from the ghostly positions in which they were frozen by the Blizzard.

Winds and high seas hurled several boats against piers, crushing them. In one bizarre incident at Lewes Harbor a tug rammed through a pier, severing the dock in half. The tug's crew abandoned ship by jumping on to the outer end of the pier. Minutes later, a wrecking steamer was forced through the breach between pilings opened by the tug. Her crew also jumped, joining those already marooned on the tottering pier. Within an hour each sailor was sheeted with a coating of ice. Fearing that any sudden movement would cause the wharf to collapse, the eleven apparitions clung to the shattered dock for 23 hours, tantalizingly close to shore but completely cut off.

Debris from ships wrecked during the Blizzard litters the beach at Lewes Harbor, along with a pilot schooner that washed ashore. Crews manning the life-saving station at left were helpless to rescue sailors aboard storm-tossed ships in the harbor. (Delaware State Archives)

Four of the six crew members of the schooner *Alice Belden* were saved in a thrilling rescue at Lewes Harbor. Buffeted by heavy winds, the ship, which had sailed earlier in the week from Maine with the ironic cargo of ice, ran aground on a sand bar during the first night of the storm and capsized. The crew scampered into the rigging and remained perched above the sinking vessel. Attempts to reach them by a shore-based lifesaving crew and another tug were futile. As two hundred spectators gawked in horror from the shore, the main mast to which the crew members clung snapped in the gale. Miraculously, the mast was kept from falling into the raging sea by the spring stay, a rope connecting the schooner's two masts. As the main mast swayed closer to the fore mast, the half-frozen sailors crept one by one into the forward rigging. Just as the last sailor moved to the forward perch, the spring stay snapped sending the entire main mast into the tempestuous waters.

*Schooners lay twisted and capsized in Lewes Harbor, Delaware, following the Blizzard. (Connecticut State Library)*

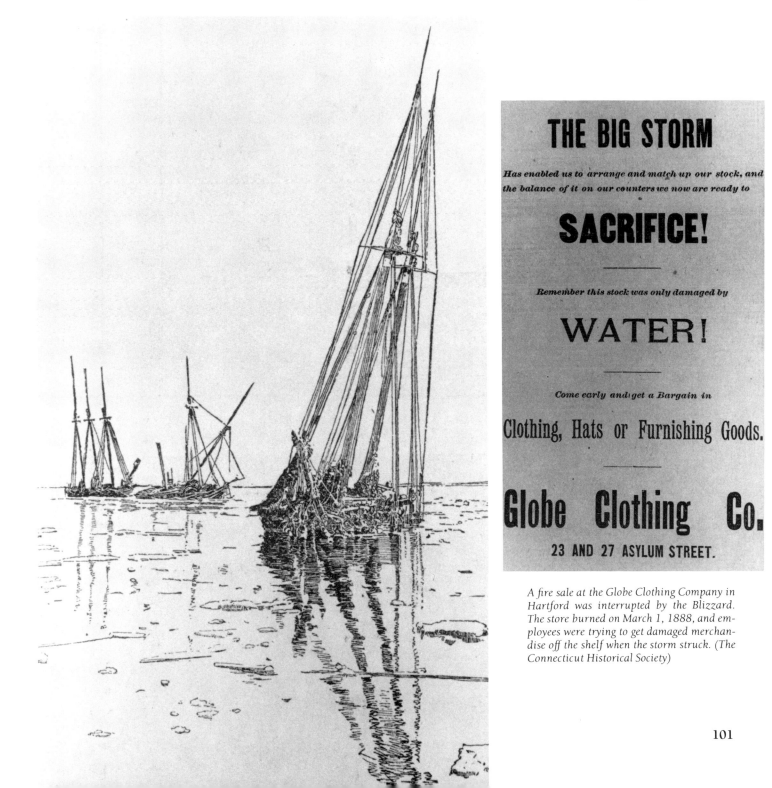

*A fire sale at the Globe Clothing Company in Hartford was interrupted by the Blizzard. The store burned on March 1, 1888, and employees were trying to get damaged merchandise off the shelf when the storm struck. (The Connecticut Historical Society)*

Harper's Weekly *drew this engraving depicting the wreck of the* Lizzie Crawford *from the photograph below. (Connecticut State Library)*

*The crew of the tug* Lizzie Crawford *abandoned ship when the steam-powered vessel crashed through a pier at Lewes Harbor during the Blizzard. The sailors shivered on the shattered dock for 23 hours without protection from the howling wind until a rescue team could reach them. (Delaware State Archives)*

Minutes later, one benumbed sailor lost his grip and tumbled into the icy waters to drown. A second climbed down the mast and urged his comrades to join him in a desperate swim to shore. He vacillated at the rail for a moment, unable to decide whether to jump. A frigid wave lurched over the bow and washed the hesitant mariner overboard, never to be seen again. After a lengthy battle against the wind and high seas, a small skiff finally arrived to take the men off the stricken schooner. The crew of the *Alice Belden*, suspended above the angry sea by a fragile web of ropes that held the ship's sails, had spent a total of twelve hours fighting the storm.

The oyster fleets on Chesapeake Bay suffered substantial damage. In the Annameesex River, an arm of the bay near Baltimore, local residents tried to rescue a foundering schooner. The storm kept the rescuers at bay until subsiding on Wednesday. When the vessel was finally boarded, they discovered a grisly scene. All six crew members, overcome by the extreme cold, were frozen stiff where they had fallen unconscious.

All along the shores of Delaware, Maryland and Virginia, coastal communities were inundated by high seas. Shore dwellers took refuge in attics and prayed that buildings stay erect on feeble foundations as sea water swirled around the lower floors. In a few locations, boats were carried inland as much as 500 feet and left high and dry when the tides receded. Newspaper accounts estimated that more than 200 vessels were sunk or damaged beyond repair and dozens of lives lost in the storm.

## Havoc on the High Seas

Wind-blown seas made sport of ships all along the east coast. In an era when sail-powered vessels still outnumbered those with steam engines by 10 to 1, harbor masters held little hope that many would be able to outlast the fury of the storm. Pilot boats, small vessels responsible for ushering larger craft into major harbors, were tossed about indifferently by the storm as they waited at port entrances. Just off Sandy Hook, New Jersey, a point passed by ships entering New York harbor, more than eight pilot boats were washed ashore.

One sailor aboard the pilot boat *Hope No. 1* who survived the barrage of snow and wind when his boat went ashore told a New York newspaper reporter of the suffering endured by those caught at sea:

> We were standing out off the Sandy Hook lightship when the storm struck us. It soon became apparent that the boat was unmanageable. The next thing we knew the breakers were boiling like yeast under her bow. She went ashore, and God only knows how we escaped. Seven other boats suffered a like fate. It doesn't seem possible that all the men belonging to those boats escaped alive.

Long Island Sound carried heavy traffic in coastal shipping and was the scene of many wrecks during the Blizzard of '88. A coal-laden schooner went aground on a shoal near Branford, Connecticut, ripping out her wooden bottom. The crew scrambled into a small dinghy, but it too capsized in the swell. One crew member swam and then waded to shore. Fighting frostbite, he walked to town and managed to get assistance to the other members of the crew. The captain was lost, but all other crew members somehow survived the icy ordeal.

*Sails and rigging on the schooner* Elizabeth M. Lea *are encased in ice as the vessel rides at anchor in the Delaware River at Philadelphia. Ships' logs from many sailing vessels caught in the Blizzard note that sledge hammers and axes had to be used to free canvas and ropes from imprisonment in rime ice. (Historical Society of Pennsylvania)*

Several ships foundered near East Neck on the Sound's southern shore. One monster barge bound for New York with a cargo of 300,000 bricks lost its deck and most of its cargo before running aground. When the barge got stuck, Captain John Moore and mate John Hill unleashed a small lifeboat and started for shore. It was agreed that when the lifeboat swamped, both men would jump into the surf and try to swim for shore. When the time to make the leap came, the mate lost his footing and was dragged out by the undertow. Captain Moore was more fortunate and reached dry land, more dead than alive, after crawling on hands and knees through the crashing surf. The mate's body washed up a short time later completely encased in ice. Three other barges were thrown high and dry on the same beach by the storm's end. One tore its hull open by crashing into the grounded brick-laden barge.

Aboard Pilot Boat No. 13 just outside New York harbor, William Inglis, a reporter for the *New York World*, was acutely aware of the boiling seas and the need for prayers for seamen trapped in the storm. He hoped that someone was praying for him because he was far too seasick to do so himself. More than once the 85-foot schooner had been lifted completely out of the water by the waves, only to have the sea surge over the decks and through the hatch when the ship came crashing down.

After a long struggle, the crew managed to set a sail that would help the vessel hold a bit closer to the wind and avoid the disastrous action of waves hitting the ship abeam. With his hands clamped on his queasy stomach, Inglis asked the captain what the chances were that the ship and crew would survive the storm.

"My lad," said the dry-witted captain, "We must put our trust in Providence, even if we do come ashore at Newport."

On Wednesday, the seas quieted and the crew sat down to its first regular meal in three days. As the crew began eating, the sailor on watch hailed a passing tug. "What news?" he called.

"Nine pilot boats lost with all hands," shouted the sailor on the tug. In the cabin below, the senior pilot pushed his plate aside and went on deck. Inglis saw tears in the old salt's eyes as he passed.

While most ships rode out the storm at sea, a few managed to make landfall and tie up at docks. Among them was a passenger vessel bound for New York carrying immigrants from Lithuania. When passenger H. N. Davidsohn strode down the gangplank into the storm, he concluded that the Blizzard was the natural climate of the terrain where he was about to make his new home. He plaintively moaned that he might as well have chosen to emigrate to Siberia.

A collision with the breakwater or another ship smashed the stern of this vessel in Lewes Harbor. (Delaware State Archives)

Draft horses pulled small boats through the streets of Brooklyn delivering coal to chilly homeowners who failed to anticipate the Blizzard.

# Chapter 6 — The Business of the Blizzard

**B**ooms and panics were a way of life on Wall Street during the 19th century. In 1884, a minor financial panic sent the stock market into a tailspin. By the time the Blizzard struck, however, the market had long since recovered and reflected America's optimism about the future of the economy. An estimated 1,000,000 Americans were stockholders. New York was well established as the nation's financial center, and its newspapers avidly reported business news for investors. The public, though, remained chary of the barons of finance who wielded power on the Street in the 1880s. In many minds, the piracy on the high seas practiced by Captain Kidd and his crew during Wall Street's early years had only changed in style. Chicanery and stock-watering schemes by financiers, brokers and the moguls of industry were viewed as business as usual.

## The View From Wall Street

The communications revolution that began with Samuel Morse's sputtering telegraph in 1840 exploded with Bell's invention of the telephone in 1876. Wall Street was swift to adopt the new technology, and communication between brokers, investors, and the exchanges was almost instantaneous. The ubiquitous ticker with its miles of paper tape announced the latest transactions. Brokers were able to gauge the trend and execute dozens of orders simultaneously. Reliant on the new technology, the New York Stock Exchange was virtually knocked out when the Blizzard downed telegraph and telephone lines.

Wall Street had already experienced its ''Black Thursday'' and ''Black Friday,'' but a ''White Monday''? With Mother Nature responsible? The first day of the Blizzard took a heavy toll on the Stock Exchange. At the opening bell, the trading floor looked like a deserted ballroom with just 30 of the 1,100 members present. Instead of the shouts of brokers and the clatter of tickers, the loudest noise was the howl of the wind through the telegraph wires outside. Only five stocks were traded, and volume totaled a mere 15,200 shares, a far cry from the normal weekday trading activity of 150,000 to 200,000 shares.

*A snow-clogged Fulton Street in lower Manhattan. (The New York Historical Society)*

Ironically, the drop in stock prices on Monday was largely the result of financial — not weather — news. In a market dominated by transportation issues, there was considerable worry over the liability for a fatal crash completely unrelated to the storm involving a passenger train on the Erie Railroad. The phenomenally bad quarterly earnings report of the New York and New England Railroad also bothered traders. And the continuing strike against the Chicago, Burlington & Quincy, which threatened to touch off strikes against other lines in the midwest, added to Wall Street's depressed mood. Not until a few days later, when investors assessed the impact on the railroads of clean-up and repair costs, did the storm enter their minds.

Tuesday's Exchange activity was even lighter. A mere 2,000 shares changed hands, probably the lowest volume on record. The board of directors quickly passed a motion to suspend trading for the day, and an impromptu baseball game between the few rival brokers who showed up took over the trading floor. A heavy cane and a ball of yarn served as the bat and ball.

The New York commodity markets showed similar inactivity owing to a shortage of traders and total cutoff of essential communications. Business was suspended at the produce exchange because one of the three men required to open the vault's triple combination lock was buried in the drifts on a train somewhere in New Jersey, beyond the reach of telegraph or telephone. Exchange officials sought assistance from steamship operators to postpone sailings for week because it would be impossible to deliver goods according to contract.

*Hand labor was the only method to clear the streets. This crew worked on 6th Avenue near 12th Street. (The New York Historical Society)*

*Newspapers like the New York Morning Journal brought out special editions to satisfy news-starved readers. (The New York Historical Society)*

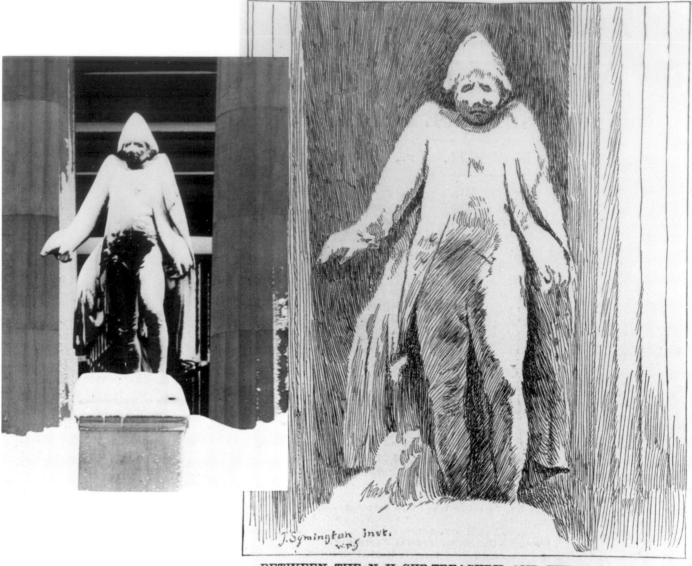

**BETWEEN THE N. Y. SUB-TREASURY AND THE SNOW-DRIFT.**
With a surplus of coin in the vaults below,
And above and around a surplus of snow,
No wonder "G. W." stands opprest
By problems that weigh on his l(e)aden breast.

*Photographer Richard Lawrence captured the essence of the Blizzard's effect on Wall Street with this image of George Washington's statue atop a pyramid of snow. Engraver J. Symington created the woodcut from Lawrence's photograph for* Harper's Weekly. *Four lines of doggerel caption the woodcut: "With a surplus of coin in the vaults below,/ And above and around a surplus of snow,/No wonder 'G. W.' stands opprest/ By problems that weigh on his l(e)aden breast." (Photo: The New York Historical Society. Engraving: Connecticut State Library)*

After the storm was over, the statue of George Washington across from the corner of Wall and Broad Streets surveyed an eerie scene. Its face caked with snow, the landmark stood atop the summit of a smooth pyramid of snow on the Treasury building's steps that no one would dare climb. The financial district looked like a whitened ghost town. Snow-laden telegraph wires filigreed the sky. White drifts were banked against second story windows. Telegraph poles appeared as masts of spectral clipper ships frozen in the Bering Sea.

By Wednesday, the stock market's pace started to pick up. A total of 106,000 shares changed hands, about half of the normal volume. Almost all of the orders came from either local or overseas traders; telegraph links with the rest of the United States were still ruptured. Activity on the commodity exchanges was still lackluster. The most excitement of the day was found on Wall Street itself when a sled carrying two tons of silver bullion valued at $80,000 lost a runner, overturned and dumped its precious cargo into a huge snow drift in front of the Treasury building. The six guards assigned to the wagon furiously dug the silver bars out of the snow with bare hands.

The Blizzard paralyzed New York's wholesale merchandise district to even more of an extent than the stock market. Entirely dependent on truckers and their horsedrawn carts and wagons for deliveries, wholesalers had loaded goods in the early hours before the Blizzard hit. At dawn, however, with the snow already falling lickety-split, many truckers refused to hitch their teams to the loaded wagons. Those who ventured into the streets soon found teams overwhelmed at the prospect of pulling a loaded cart through the windswept snow. Many carts were abandoned, blocking streets and creating new barriers against which drifts could accumulate. The lucky ones left their carts at the loading dock.

Retailers took a severe knock from the storm, too. Many large department stores, including Macy & Co., Lord & Taylor and Denning & Co. in New York, had planned showings on Monday of new spring fashions. Only a fraction of the normal staff of sales clerks waited for customers, but buyers were almost nowhere to be seen. At B. Altman, only one customer passed through the doors all day — an old woman who battled the snow to purchase two spools of thread.

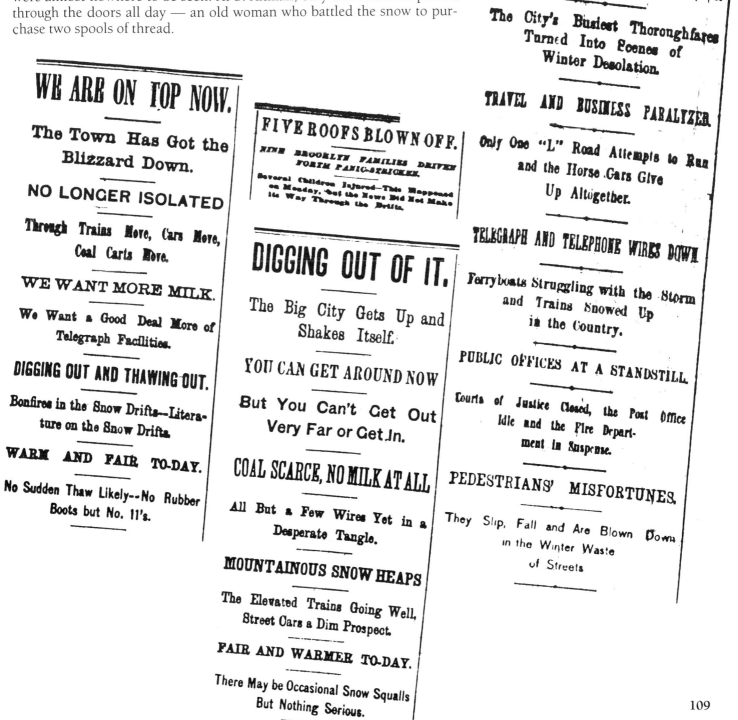

## SNOWBOUND.

### New York's Mighty Pulse Almost Stilled by a Terrible Storm.

#### RAGING WIND AND BLINDING DRIFT.

The City's Busiest Thoroughfares Turned Into Scenes of Winter Desolation.

#### TRAVEL AND BUSINESS PARALYZED.

Only One "L" Road Attempts to Run and the Horse Cars Give Up Altogether.

#### TELEGRAPH AND TELEPHONE WIRES DOWN

Ferryboats Struggling with the Storm and Trains Snowed Up in the Country.

#### PUBLIC OFFICES AT A STANDSTILL.

Courts of Justice Closed, the Post Office Idle and the Fire Department in Suspense.

#### PEDESTRIANS' MISFORTUNES.

They Slip, Fall and Are Blown Down in the Winter Waste of Streets

## WE ARE ON TOP NOW.

### The Town Has Got the Blizzard Down.

#### NO LONGER ISOLATED

Through Trains Move, Cars Move, Coal Carts Move.

#### WE WANT MORE MILK.

We Want a Good Deal More of Telegraph Facilities.

#### DIGGING OUT AND THAWING OUT.

Bonfires in the Snow Drifts--Literature on the Snow Drifts.

#### WARM AND FAIR TO-DAY.

No Sudden Thaw Likely--No Rubber Boots but No. 11's.

## FIVE ROOFS BLOWN OFF.

### NINE BROOKLYN FAMILIES DRIVEN FORTH PANIC-STRICKEN.

Several Children Injured--This Happened on Monday, but the News Did Not Make its Way Through the Drifts.

## DIGGING OUT OF IT.

### The Big City Gets Up and Shakes Itself.

#### YOU CAN GET AROUND NOW

But You Can't Get Out Very Far or Get In.

#### COAL SCARCE, NO MILK AT ALL

All But a Few Wires Yet in a Desperate Tangle.

#### MOUNTAINOUS SNOW HEAPS

The Elevated Trains Going Well, Street Cars a Dim Prospect.

#### FAIR AND WARMER TO-DAY.

There May be Occasional Snow Squalls But Nothing Serious.

*Scenes of the Blizzard in New York City are depicted in these engravings from the March 24, 1888 issue of* Scientific American. *At top left: Marooned passengers aboard elevated railway cars make their way to the street on rickety ladders. Right: Abandoned and derailed horsecars and horsedrawn wagons litter Broadway. Bottom left: Track clearing efforts result in a wrecked locomotive in Jersey City. (Connecticut State Library)*

Snow drifted in front of Macy's main entrance as fast as maintenance workers could shovel it out. It made little difference; the sales clerks who managed to get in to work far outnumbered the customers. When closing time arrived, the managers invited saleswomen who lived too far to walk home to stay in the store overnight. Mattresses and cots were brought out of inventory, and everything necessary to make the women comfortable was provided. Male sales clerks had to fend for themselves in the icy blast.

## Did You Hear The One About The Traveling Salesman?

For the ill-prepared merchant coming to New York from a distant city, business during the Blizzard was anything but usual. Accompanied by his business partner, A. C. Chadbourne arrived in Manhattan as the storm was reaching its peak intensity:

> I left Boston on the midnight train Sunday, March 11 for New York. The weather had been mild and I was attired in a cutaway coat, patent leather shoes, lightweight top coat and the proverbial silk hat which all young men wore at that period. I awoke at 7 a.m. . . . looked out the car window and found the train was stalled in deep snow at about 127th Street. I got out the car door and saw a line of cars and trains stalled ahead of me as far as one could see down the tracks.

> I talked the matter over with my partner and two husky looking traveling men and they decided to follow my lead over to Third Avenue, expecting to get an elevated train down to 42nd Street. There were some stone steps thoroughly snow covered leading from the elevated tracks of the New Haven Railroad down to the sidewalk. Down these steps we slid, landing in a snow bank at the bottom which nearly buried us alive. . . . Great drifts were piled six to eight feet high in many places and the air was so full of snow it was difficult to see where one was going. We continued wallowing along until we reached 125th Street and Third Avenue, only to find that no trains were running on the elevated tracks.

We discovered a small restaurant . . . into which we filed for much needed food. About two doors below I saw a small shop open. . . . I purchased two pairs of thin woolen hose, four pairs of the heaviest, largest size woolen hose he had and two bandanna handkerchiefs. Returning to the restaurant we took off our wet patent leather shoes and stockings and sat barefoot drying off our feet and trousers around the coal stove while beefsteaks and fried potatoes were prepared for our breakfast. We put on the thin woolen hose while our shoes dried. We pulled the coarse woolen hose over our shoes, tucked our trousers in them and tied the hose around our ankles with cord to keep the snow from working down into our feet. We tied the bandanna handkerchiefs over our heads and under our chins and then pulled our silk hats as far down on our heads as possible. The two other pairs of hose we pulled on over our gloves in place of mittens and thus attired we started south.

There was a heavy gale blowing. I remember seeing my partner blown helplessly almost a block, his travel ended by a fall into a snow drift which completely buried him. We overtook a milk wagon drawn by two powerful dapple gray horses. Neither my partner or myself had very much cash with us but we made up a pool . . . and offered the driver $50 to get us down to 42nd Street. Although the milk wagon was small and empty, he refused, stating that he would be thankful if he got his horses back to the stable alive. . . . Perhaps a half-mile farther we overtook the milk wagon [again] with one of the big horses down, buried in the snow and apparently dead, and the other one showing great distress from fatigue. I helped the driver unharness the live horse and left them to their fate.

We finally reached 42nd Street, where in passing a vacant corner lot we narrowly escaped death . . . [when] a wooden fence . . . was blown on to us while wallowing in a deep drift. It was with the greatest difficulty that we worked our way west . . . to the Old St. Cloud Hotel, then situated at the corner of Broadway and 42nd Street.

*A milkman uses oxen to pull a sled filled with milk cans on East Main Street in Meriden, Connecticut. (Meriden Historical Society)*

The task of shoveling a path through drifts higher than their heads in front of uptown Manhattan brownstones confronted these two laborers. (Connecticut State Library)

Chadbourne stayed only for a few minutes in the St. Cloud's bar before embarking on the final four-block journey to his destination, the Gedney House at 38th Street and Broadway, where he had reservations and knew the manager.

I distinctly remember being blown down twice while crossing Broadway and crawling through the snow on my hands and knees on the west sidewalk of Broadway. [Entering the hotel] I observed my good friend Mr. Brue in back of the desk. I walked up to him and said, "Hello, for Heaven's sake give us a couple of rooms and a bath."

Friend Brue looked at me and said, "I am very sorry, sir, but there is not a vacant bed in the house. All I can offer you is a couple of chairs in the office here to which you are welcome at no expense."

I pulled off my hat and said, "It is pretty darn tough, Brue, when you cannot find a place for an old friend."

He looked at me a second time and said, "My God! It's Chadbourne. Look in the mirror if you want a sight."

I knew my partner looked terribly, his mustache was a wabbly cake of ice which had pounded on his chin as he walked until his chin was bleeding. My face was scratched, red as a lobster, my eyebrows were frozen and my chin was resting on a cake of snowy ice packed in between the top of my overcoat and my bandanna handkerchief.

By the time we got our coats and woolen hose off and got the snow and ice brushed off our clothing, Mr. Brue came down and told us to come up to his apartment. He had a bed put up in his own parlor where an open fire was burning brightly.

Money was scarce and the hotel was soon filled with checks and I.O.U.s. The train bearing my suitcase arrived at Grand Central Station early Thursday morning and on Friday my partner and I started for Philadelphia.

Competition was keen among photographers eager to sell Blizzard souvenir photographs. A. L. Butler sold his work in Hartford, Connecticut. (The Connecticut Historical Society)

## A Losing Proposition

The Blizzard dealt the railroads severe financial losses. Lost revenue from ticket sales and the enormous cost of cleanup combined to bring havoc to balance sheets and send shivers up the spines of stockholders and those who owned railroad mortgage bonds. A week after the storm, Acting President Reed of the Consolidated Railroad, a line that served much of Connecticut, said that the Blizzard caused the worst red ink for the railroad in 34 years. He estimated that $15,000 had been spent every day since the storm ended to remove snow from the tracks.

Telegraph companies were hard hit, too. Rerouting of telegraph communications made some roundabout connections necessary. Direct communication between Boston and Concord, New Hampshire, for example, a distance of about 50 miles, lasted only until Monday at 1 p.m. when lines and poles blew down like tomato stakes in the wind. Boston-bound telegrams were then sent through the still operating wires via Worcester and Springfield, Massachusetts, until those lines went dead as well. Undaunted, telegraph operators turned their attention north sending Boston's messages to Montreal. Canadian telegraph operators then forwarded them to Boston on a line that was still working. By nightfall, this arrangement collapsed as the Montreal office announced that it could not handle the volume of traffic it was asked to transmit.

"How odd that the only uninterrupted line of communication between New York and the outside world was under the ocean with Europe," editorialized the *New York Herald*. For 24 hours, it was easier to reach London than Yonkers or New Rochelle. Only the wires of the Commercial Cable Company, the firm that owned and operated the trans-Atlantic cable to London, were working by mid-afternoon on the first day of the Blizzard. The storm paralyzed Western Union's domestic links out of the city. Commercial Cable stayed in operation during the Blizzard because the entire cable in Manhattan and Brooklyn to the link with the undersea cable at Coney Island was underground. Western Union's wires were almost exclusively above ground and very susceptible to wind and ice damage. The advantage of underground cable placement was not lost on frustrated telegraph operators and those who tried to send messages.

*A plow sits on a sidetrack at the Springfield, Massachusetts, depot. (Springfield Public Library)*

*Deeply drifted snow in a rock cut snared these Connecticut Western Railroad engines. The ghost-like image in front of the locomotive is a shoveler who moved too fast to be caught by the camera. (The Connecticut Historical Society)*

As the number of downed wires continued to mount, damage estimates escalated rapidly. A few days after the storm, the trade journal *Electric Age* reckoned that $100,000 would not be enough to cover Western Union's damaged lines. The full extent of the damage was not assessed until two weeks later when the same periodical noted:

> "The Western Union wires particularly are in wretched condition. The recent storm played sad havoc with them, necessitating a practical rebuilding of the system between Washington and Boston. The loss to the company was immense. . . . The recent blizzard has taught the telegraph, telephone and electric light companies the necessity of placing their wires underground as speedily as possible."

Days before the storm, Western Union released a financial report for the quarter ending December 31, 1887, showing very poor earnings of just $55,000. Coupled with news of storm-related damage to the company's facilities, stockholders turned bearish, sending Western Union stock down three points the following week and into a slow downward spiral for the next few months.

## Neither Rain, Nor Snow, Nor Gloom of Night?

The loss of telegraph service was damaging enough to commerce, but the loss of mail service owing to the Blizzard had a greater impact on ordinary citizens. Postal delivery service in most communities was suspended during the storm, and streets and roads made impassable by drifts curtailed extensive deliveries for several days. Those carriers who braved the wind and snow had precious little to deliver anyway; the intercity trains that carried the mail were stuck in the drifts.

Overnight mail delivery between most cities in the northeastern states was taken for granted in the 1880s. An efficient network of rail transportation throughout the area made it possible. A letter posted at noon in Manchester, New Hampshire, typically reached a recipient in St. Albans, Vermont, on the next business day or two. The Blizzard extended that trip for a week, with letters mailed on March 8 arriving March 15.

Only two trains arrived in New York with mail on Monday. Deliveries were attempted in the city, but most mail was brought back to the post office because few businesses were open to receive it. Postmen in Brooklyn who tried to make their appointed rounds suffered from severe frostbite and exposure. More than 20 mail carriers in that city alone had to be rescued when they fell on ice-coated steps or got mired in drifts.

*A stately elm tree toppled by the wind crashed into the third-floor windows of a residence on Fairfield Avenue in Bridgeport, Connecticut. (Bridgeport Public Library)*

*Nine days after the storm, street clearing operations were still ongoing in New Haven, Connecticut. Here, workers load a wagon with Blizzard debris in front of the post office in a photograph dated March 21, 1888. (New Haven Colony Historical Society)*

# Chapter 7 — *The Aftermath*

The Blizzard of 88's violence would have turned any day of the week into a disaster. Its arrival on a Monday morning was cataclysmic. The disruption in the food distribution system could not have happened at a worse time. Grocers traditionally used Monday to replenish stocks depleted by weekend shopping. When the Blizzard upset the food chain by severing the fragile link from producers, retailers could not obtain fresh supplies.

In 1888, families in cities depended on fresh meat, produce and dairy products each day. Other than the wooden ice box, refrigeration was unknown and food could not be easily preserved. A trip to the green grocer or butcher, or a visit from dealers who sold such products from push carts, was therefore part of the daily schedule.

In the laissez-faire economy of 1888, the law of supply and demand operated with a cruel reality. As a commodity got scarcer and demand grew, the price was quickly adjusted upward. In Newark, New Jersey, for example, prices appreciated almost as fast as the snow drifts. Eggs were sold for 35 to 40 cents per dozen on the day after the Blizzard, double the normal price. Steak jumped from 25 to 50 cents a pound. A can of condensed milk that sold for 13 cents on Monday cost 25 cents on Tuesday and 35 cents on Wednesday.

## The Threat of Famine

During the height of the Blizzard on Monday, a gardener named Jack Mangin left a cozy spot next to the stove in his favorite saloon on Staten Island, New York, to go home for rubber boots. On arrival, he discovered a deep drift blocking the door. Mangin trudged back to the saloon for a shovel, slung it over his shoulder, and faced the wind and snow once again for the walk back to his house.

"John," screamed a woman from a second story window as he passed by, "won't you please get somebody to help you and dig us out!"

*Visiting the local tavern was a long difficult walk through the drifts in Huntington, New York. (Huntington Historical Society)*

"You are better off inside," replied the gardener, shouting over the din of the wind. "I had to go a half a mile for a shovel to dig myself in."

"But we have nothing to eat!"

"Well, ma'am, Lent isn't over yet, and as sure as you live this is a fast day," said the gardener as he vanished amid the snowflakes.

Both the pious and agnostic went hungry during the Blizzard of '88. Families with small children began to suffer before the snow stopped falling because of a total lack of fresh milk in most areas affected by the storm. In New York alone, some 600,000 to 700,000 quarts of milk were consumed every day. Not a drop flowed into the city from Monday until Wednesday, and even then the meager supply could not possibly keep pace with demand. Grocers with a supply of canned condensed milk did a thriving business and stocks were soon depleted. Many milk dealers refused to serve their regular customers and routes because of fears that their horses were not up to the task of pulling a milk cart through snow-clogged streets. As supplies dried up and milk became a precious commodity, grocers demanded and got 10 to 15 cents for a quart, far in excess of the two or three cents usually paid. One New York milkman who did manage to make his rounds drove his sled along a 20-foot high drift on East 59th St. to make deliveries through the second-story windows.

*A team of four oxen haul a milk sled on Main Street in Hartford. (The Connecticut Historical Society)*

(Copyrighted.)

## The Great Clinton Street Drift and Tunnel,

HARTFORD, CONN.

Height of Tunnel, 6 ft. 3 in.
Height of Drift at arch, 10 ft.
Height of Drift at house, 15 ft.

Photograph taken two days
after the storm of March 13-14,
1888.

*Photographer J. H. Eckhardt of Hartford, Connecticut, sought to protect the copyright on his images by warning the public to accept no imitations of his work. This advertisement appeared in the Hartford Times a week after the storm. (The Connecticut Historical Society)*

*The fading light of the afternoon sun casts long shadows on The Great Clinton Street Drift and Tunnel in Hartford, Connecticut. Dug through a ten-foot high drift, the tunnel had six feet, three inches of clearance. At its peak against the house at the right, the drift was 15 feet deep. The photo was taken two days after the snow stopped falling. (The Connecticut Historical Society)*

The situation was similar in almost all snowbound communities. The problem lay not with the supply — the cows sat contentedly in barns during the storm anticipating the twice-a-day touch of farm hands — but in the distribution system that had been totally disrupted by the storm. In Poughkeepsie, New York, dairy farmer George Deuell barely kept up with the flood of milk that his cows continued to produce, which he could not get to market. In his diary, Deuell's son wrote:

> Pa doesn't know what to do with his milk as he cannot take it off and it shows no sign of clearing off and even if it does clear off there is no knowing how soon we can get through the drifts. He would gladly give it to the cows if they would drink it. They will not drink it. He hasn't got enough cans now that so many are filled with milk.

A few days later another diary entry notes that much of the overabundant milk supply on the Deuell farm got churned into butter for the family's use. By the Saturday after the Blizzard, roads around the farm had been cleared enough to permit a horsedrawn wagon to bring a supply of milk to a distribution point in Wasaic, New York. Arriving there, the Deuells found that a train wreck near the Sharon station had blocked the tracks and no consignments for the milk train were being accepted. Not until March 31, three weeks after the storm, did Deuell find a firm market for his farm's products.

B. C. Patterson, a dairy farmer and milkman in Torrington, Connecticut, milked his cows as usual during the Blizzard and warehoused it in the cold storage vaults Mother Nature had so graciously provided. He sold 500 quarts of milk walking door to door the day after the storm. Almost every family who saw him on the street purchased the precious commodity as he passed by. Distribution was hindered greatly because milk wagons could not traverse snow-clogged streets. The civic-minded (some say profit-minded) Patterson hired shoveling crews at his own expense to clear the way for his horse drawn carts.

A purchasing clerk's error helped avoid hunger at the New York Infant Asylum in Westchester County. Normally eight cans of milk were supplied each day by a dairy located eight miles away, enough to feed 400 orphaned or unwanted children between the ages of two weeks and six years and 200 unwed mothers-to-be normally housed there. The Blizzard changed all that, isolating the institution for a full week. A few days before the storm, however, a large supply of Borden's canned condensed milk had arrived. Instead of the 12 dozen cans ordered, 12 gross or 1,728 cans were delivered. The resident physician, Dr. Charles Gilmore Kerley, had reservations about how bottle-fed infants would react to the condensed product. Diluted with barley water, it was given to the children with positive results. Babies who had been difficult to feed began to gain weight. The forced experiment strongly influenced Dr. Kerley's thinking about infant nutrition. For the next 50 years, he advocated the use of evaporated milk for infant feeding.

*The sidewalks were clear, but the streets were buried under a deep blanket of snow in Derby, Connecticut. This photograph shows Main Street looking west. Note the well-dressed gentleman with western-style cowboy boots standing in the doorway at right. (Derby Public Library)*

## No Meat Today

Meat supplies were just as hard to come by as dairy products. One Trumbull, Connecticut, woman's diary tells how her father and brother "cannot get a bit of beef in B-port [Bridgeport, Connecticut]" on the Saturday after the storm. Butchers didn't resume their regular deliveries in Trumbull until a week after the flakes began to fall.

*Deep snow on John Street in Worcester, Massachusetts. (American Antiquarian Society)*

*Looking up Broad Street in Bridgeport, Connecticut. (Bridgeport Public Library)*

REMOVING THE DRIFTS.

Worcester, Tuesday, March 13.

*The weather to-day is likely to be fair and colder, or stormy and hotter.*

119

# SIGNS OF SPRING.

NEW YORK AS IT LOOKED AFTER THE STORM

**EVERYBODY SNOWED UNDER BUT THE GLOBE TELEPHONE MAN.**

Beef supplies in most cities were probably close to normal at meat wholesalers. Getting sides of beef cut and delivered to the corner grocer was the problem. Animals caught in transit between the farm and the meat packing plant suffered immensely, however. Thousands of cattle froze to death while trapped in railroad cars. There were reports that pigs caught in the Blizzard's clutches on the way to market went into a cannibalistic frenzy when deprived of feed for several days.

Few butchers in New York City tried to service their regular customers during the storm, causing problems for restaurants, especially those in hotels where many stranded commuters had sought refuge. One dealer got two loads of meat from markets in lower Manhattan to a midtown restaurant on a bobsled and vowed it was more successful than a trip in a wagon or sleigh would have been. Another enterprising meat purveyor tossed a haunch of beef across the back of a horse and led the animal up the street. That mode of conveyance was easier than trying to navigate a wagon through the drifts. The butcher simply cut what his customers wanted on the street, charging what the traffic would bear. Uptown Manhattan markets quickly doubled their meat prices. Despite the grumbles of customers, few refused to submit to the exacting prices demanded by butchers.

120

The snow drifted to a height of 12 feet in front of a Hartford, Connecticut, home where a dozen strangers had taken refuge with a family. No one was able to exit or enter the home for four days until a tunnel could be dug through the drift blocking the front door. The occupants were not without company — hundreds of sparrows had also taken refuge and become trapped under the home's back porch. When the larder was emptied and hunger pangs began to rumble through the stomachs of the trapped residents, the sparrows were gathered up and turned into sparrow pie.

Seafood was also in short supply. Fishing boats stayed in port throughout the storm and many captains spent the days after the storm repairing damage to boats buffeted by the wind and waves. The Fulton Street fish wholesalers were unable to obtain new supplies to replace those sold over the weekend preceding the storm. At least one fishmonger saw an obligation to help avoid hunger. Charles Philipsen of the North River Fish and Game Company contacted New York's Police Superintendent Murray asking where 500 pounds of fish might be given to families in need. Officers at the Oak Street police station distributed the fish to seventy needy families.

*A solitary wooden snow shovel rests against a pile of snow about eight feet high along Main Street in Northampton, Massachusetts. (Northampton Historical Society)*

## An Energy Crisis

*The Anthony Novelette, a 5″ x 7″ format field camera, was highly prized by photographers at the time of the Blizzard. The company which produced it, Edward Anthony, had manufactured cameras and photographic supplies since 1842, the first American firm to serve photographers. (Wayne Cogan Collection)*

Disruptions in train schedules left many people out in the cold right inside their own homes. Coal was the most popular fuel for home heating in 1888. Nearly every homeowner reserved a corner of the basement for the coal bin and kept it well stocked during the winter months. The relatively mild winter and signs of spring that preceded the Blizzard lulled many homeowners into complacency about keeping the coal bin filled. When temperatures plunged down to zero and frigid winds rattled window panes, most were unable to get additional supplies delivered from the coal yards.

Poor families suffered even more. In drafty tenements throughout major cities, destitute families had cut the cold by filling coal stoves on a day-to-day basis. Their fuel wasn't delivered by the half-ton in wagons pulled by huge draft horses. Most likely, it was the responsibility of an eight- to ten-year old child to visit the corner grocer with a bucket each day and buy several pounds of coal, or scrounge around near railroad tracks looking for droppings from tenders. When grocers were shut off from their supplies, the price of coal skyrocketed. Many families suddenly found themselves unable to heat their rooms or cook their meals.

Electric utilities were hard pressed to keep up service to their customers, even when transmission lines remained intact. In New York City, The Brush Electric Light Company told police that they would turn off street lamps and service to customers at midnight on the first night of the storm. The coal-fired generating plant had problems obtaining enough fuel because snow-clogged streets prevented deliveries. Prospects for additional supplies were bleak as well. The railroads serving the coal mining areas in Pennsylvania were also blocked.

*Many of the residents of Forestville, Connecticut, turned out to pose for the photographer with this little engine that couldn't. (Bristol Historical Society)*

As the fuel distribution system broke down, storm-related energy problems worked their way back to producers as well as consumers. Coal burned in New York's furnaces and stoves came from eastern Pennsylvania's coal belt — towns like Reading, Wilkes-Barre and Pottsville. With no way to move their inventory, coal mine owners were forced to stop production. At the Reading Coal and Iron Company alone, 31 collieries were shut down, forcing the layoff of thousands of miners.

## Cleaning Up

At the time of the Blizzard of 1888, massive snow removal was unknown. Cities and towns usually appointed a Snow Warden or other municipal official to insure that thoroughfares were kept passable. The job consisted primarily of supervising crews to shovel snow off roads or cover up bare spots with snow to permit passage of sleighs. Often officials just let the snow amass and pack down for the convenience of runner-equipped vehicles. The covered bridge, a favorite stopping place for courting couples and a fixture of the New England landscape at that time, was repeatedly the bane of the Snow Warden's existence because the snow needed for passage of vehicles with runners could not accumulate on the roadbed.

In the mid-1880s, the snow roller became a familiar sight in northern cities and towns. Drawn by a team of horses, the rollers packed down the snow using huge drums six feet in diameter and eight to ten feet in width. The driver managed the reins from a high perch atop the contraption. The roller was extremely efficient and left a flat trail of hard-packed snow on streets where it was used. Roads between towns and villages, however, were usually left untouched; man and horse had the choice of fighting through or turning back.

Although a single snowflake seems weightless, the aching back and sore muscles of someone who has just finished shoveling Blizzard debris is a painful reminder that removing snow — lots of it — requires long hours of hard work. For example, to clear a sidewalk five feet wide and 100 feet long of 15 inches of snow, you must lift two tons more or less, depending on the proportion of air and water in the snow. That roofs sag, bend and creak under the weight of a substantial snowfall is not surprising. The roof of a moderate-sized house whose surface area measures 40 by 75 feet must support almost 18,000 pounds when covered by just ten inches of snow.

*Laborers hired by the city of Hartford clear Church Street and load the snow on horse-drawn sleds. Many workers refused the prevailing wage of 17 cents an hour, demanding as much as a dollar an hour to clear Blizzard debris. (The Connecticut Historical Society)*

123

*Clearing a sidewalk in Warwick, New York. (The New York Historical Society)*

*Fashion-conscious men in Greenfield, Massachusetts, wouldn't be seen improperly attired in public, even if the task at hand was shoving tons of snow from a clogged sidewalk. (Historical Society of Greenfield)*

Clearing the thoroughfares in New York City so the normal bustle of commerce could resume was the responsibility of Street Commissioner J. H. Coleman and his street cleaning department. It would be no easy task. Coleman calculated that the Blizzard had dumped 23,000,000 cubic yards of snow on the streets of Manhattan south of 42nd Street. Horsedrawn carts had the capacity to haul about 2 cubic yards per load. Thus, he figured that more than 11,500,000 cartloads would have to be lugged away, discouraging numbers since the average snowstorm generated only 10,000 cartloads. Because the snow had packed hard and frozen solid in many places, plowing or rolling was ruled out. Removal was the only remedy. But without machinery for snow removal, that meant muscle power behind picks, shovels and other hand implements.

Every available cart in the city was hired to haul snow away and dump it off piers into the East River. City regulations, however, prohibited dumping anything in the river except from two designated bulkheads. Harbor masters and boat captains were appalled by the plan, thinking how difficult it would be for ships to dodge miniature icebergs that had the potential to punch holes in wooden hulls. The Dock and Police Commissioners sided with the shipping interests. At a City Hall conference, Mayor Hewitt noted the complaints and politely told the harbor interests that it was the only method to cope with the snow. He then urged the reluctant city officials to cooperate with Coleman's plan.

Commissioner Coleman found his task all the more difficult because many contractors had already been employed by private citizens and business owners who were willing to pay rates far in excess of those offered by the city. Dozens of contractors who had signed snow removal agreements with the city simply failed to show up. Nevertheless, by late Tuesday, some 700 carts and 1,000 men were busy on Manhattan's streets disposing of the Blizzard's legacy.

The cost of carting off such unprecedented tons of snow taxed the street cleaning department's budget. Only $25,000 had been set aside for snow removal. Emergencies like the Blizzard of '88 were simply not foreseen. Coleman noted that a small surplus in the street sweeping budget would probably cover the deficit.

The *New York Times* ran public service notices encouraging truckmen to help the city by volunteering to clear the streets without pay, but few seemed to have heeded the newspaper's call. The opportunity for turning a profit in the aftermath of the Blizzard was a far more potent motivator than any notion of civic duty.

A few days before the storm, Henry A. Smith, a street cleaning contractor in Brooklyn, received orders from the Department of City Works to put his gangs on the street for spring cleaning beginning Monday, March 12.

I made a remark to my wife to the effect that I would like to wake up on Monday morning and find six feet of snow on the ground, not anticipating that my wish would be gratified. . . . When I reached the office the following day I was informed that the Commissioner wanted to see me at once. He wanted to know what I was going to do about the removal of the snow. He wanted me to give him a figure what I would remove the snow for. I told him if he would give me a list of streets he wanted cleaned I would give him a figure. At 2 p.m. I called at his office and he asked me what I would do the work for and I told him $250,000, and he refused to sign a contract for that figure. He then called into his office a number of outside contractors and made separate bids and I finally agreed to clear Fulton Street from Brooklyn Bridge to Bedford Avenue on a basis of 10% over the actual cost. . . . The cost of Fulton Street was something like $20,000.

*A horsedrawn sled tries to navigate down State Street in New Haven. (New Haven Colony Historical Society)*

126

The American Hotel and the Old Post Office seem dwarfed by a gigantic snow drift in downtown Hartford. (Archives, History and Genealogy Unit, Connecticut State Library)

City residents often confounded efforts to keep streets, gutters, storm drains and hydrants free of snow by careless tossing of snow cleared from sidewalks. They tackled the job with all sorts of implements. Curious old wooden shovels were wielded. Iron garden tools and coal scoops were used with varying degrees of success.

Despite the hardships enforced on slum dwellers, the Blizzard brought a financial windfall to the poor. The tons of snow and the need to get rid of it as quickly as possible allowed workers to set their own fees for the back-breaking task of removing the snow. Anybody capable of lifting a shovel could expect to make at least double the normal laborer's wages. Street car companies, contractors with street cleaning companies, the railroads, and many private agencies were giving work to all comers at a minimum of two dollars a day, a fantastic sum for the time. Boys and men lucky enough to possess the proper tools extracted exorbitant sums for their labors from homeowners and shopkeepers. Ten dollars a day, enough to make the average slum dweller feel like a Vanderbilt for a while, was not an uncommon return for an enterprising shoveler. Even three days after the storm the mountains of snow still seemed as endless as the American frontier.

THE SNOW SHOVELER RETURNING FROM WORK

Italian laborers clearing off the tracks of the New England Railroad went on strike the day after the storm ended, demanding a wage of two dollars a day. The strike was settled by mid-morning with the railroad capitulating completely to their demands. Workers in Hartford, Connecticut, were offered 17 cents per hour to shovel the streets, the going rate for laborers paid by the city's street maintenance department. Many refused to work, demanding as much as a dollar an hour.

*Scrap lumber and kerosene-soaked rags were stuffed into hollows dug in drifts and set afire in an attempt to efficiently remove the snow by melting it. Despite the roaring fires, such attempts were usually futile. The little snow that was melted formed large puddles on streets where gutters and catch basins were clogged. It simply froze again to pose a different hazard — a sheer sheet of ice across the pavement. (Connecticut State Library)*

The demand for snow shovels soon exceeded the supply. Stores that had any shovels in stock after the winter retail season found their inventory speedily depleted. John J. Meisinger, a buyer for the New York department store of Edward Ridley & Sons, took delivery of a carload of snow shovels on the Saturday before the Blizzard. He remembered being called on the carpet for purchasing winter merchandise at the end of the season, only to be congratulated when the snow hit a few days later, providing a quick $1,800 profit for the store. As he told it,

> On March 1, 1888 I purchased from Wm. Topping Auctioneers in White Street a carload of unclaimed wooden snow shovels at a ridiculous low price. Many of the buyers laughed at the idea of me buying snow shovels at the end of the season, but on March 12, 1888 . . . Ridley's was the only store that had a large stock of snow shovels and sold every one the first day. Thus ended the Blizzard Sale.

In Danbury, Connecticut, the crew at Starr's Box Shop geared up to manufacturing wooden shovels to meet the demand. Snowshoes made from wooden barrel staves helped employees get to work.

Some New Yorkers attempted to remove the snow by melting it. Hollow caves were dug into drifts blocking streets. The openings were packed with scrap wood and barrel staves, and kerosene-soaked rags were stuffed into spaces between the fuel. At the touch of a match, flames roared out of the orifice like an overworked brick oven or furnace. As hot as the fires seemed, they made little impression on the snow.

BONFIRES IN THE STREETS.

128

Vast amounts of indignation were heaped upon elevated railway officials who neglected to order the cleaning of stairways leading to station platforms after clearing off the tracks. Patrons often had to wade through knee-high depths or navigate up and down icy steps where others had packed down the coating of snow. The *New York Times* chided the line's operators on its editorial page:

> The niggardly policy now pursued by the managers of the road looks only to getting the nickels of the public and cares little for the comfort and safety of its patrons. Elevated riders already suffering from the bump and sway of the typical trip certainly concurred in their disdain for the company's lack of concern for its passengers.

In many small New England towns, little or no effort was made to remove snow from the streets. Instead, teams of four to six horses dragged heavy flat-bottomed sleds across covered streets roads to pack down the snow. Concord, New Hampshire's efforts were typical. Superintendent of Roads James H. Rowall hired 100 men to break through the mounds blockading the city's streets. Teams attacked drifts eight feet deep, taxing the strength of the horses. Substantial amounts still had to be moved by hand shoveling, a slow and arduous process that resulted in aching backs and sore muscles in the strongest of workers.

*Two horses pull a sled through the streets of Middletown, Connecticut, while a horse-drawn carriage at left seems to be having a problem making headway through the snow. Tossing the snow into the center of the street, a line of shovelers seems intent on creating the state's first divided highway. (The Connecticut Historical Society)*

*Merchants in Waterbury, Connecticut, wait patiently for customers the day after the Blizzard. (The Connecticut Historical Society)*

ADT & BROTHER, PHOTOGRAPHERS,          48 AND 63 BANK ST., WATERBURY, CONN

## AFTER THE GREAT BLIZZARD,

Small towns throughout the Blizzard area found their snow removal budgets stretched to the limit. In the northern Massachusetts community of Orange, selectman W. H. Lamb told constituents that $600 had been spent for labor to clear roads in the week after the storm. An additional $400 would probably be needed before the roads were completely passable to wheeled vehicles. The total was ten times the amount usually spent for road breaking in ordinary winters.

Laborers were not the only ones who saw a chance for profits to be made from the storm. Amid the usual advertisements for patent medicines and farms for sale in the *New Hampshire Sentinel*, a two-inch ad placed by a photographer offered 43 different views of the Blizzard ready for framing.

## Thawing Out

A late winter thaw arrived a few days after the Blizzard was over, creating sloppy conditions on many city streets. Pedestrians soon found themselves up to their ankles in slush when they stepped in places that looked like hard-packed crust. Blockages of storm drains and gutters caused by careless placement of snow removed from sidewalks often compounded the problem and caused street and basement flooding.

Flooding had a more dramatic effect in upstate New York. As warmer temperatures loosened ice and runoff from the melting snow, water flowed into rivers and streams, lifting them over their banks and threatening bridge supports. One week after the Blizzard, an immense bridge that carried tracks of the West Shore Railroad across the Schoharie Creek at Fort Hunter, New York (not far from where a New York State Thruway bridge would collapse under similar circumstances almost a century later) was washed away. Downstream in Cobleskill, New York, another railroad bridge met the same fate.

*Drifted snow almost reaches the top of a watchmaker's sidewalk sign in Pittsfield, Massachusetts. (Berkshire County Historical Society)*

*Snowbound Vassar College in Poughkeepsie, New York, on the day after the Blizzard. (Dutchess County Historical Society)*

In outlying areas of eastern Long Island, snow removal and freedom from the isolation induced by the storm were slow in coming. No information about the Blizzard's deadly force reached Greenport until Thursday, March 15 when two delayed steamers sailed into the harbor. As one account suggests, the residents were as "ignorant of the doings and misdoings of the great city as though they were castaways on a great desert island." A still snowbound 11-year-old farm girl in West Neck wrote a letter a week after the first flakes fell telling about the storm's power and desolation.

The roads were so blocked up that until Wednesday nothing could be done to clear them off. Even then nothing but heavy wood sleighs could pass and those not 'til afternoon. Friday was the first day fit for any other kind of sleighs. But sleighing did not last long for yesterday we had to use a wagon. No school at all last week as it was impossible for anyone to get there no matter how near they lived. Gilbert and myself are still away from school. We do not expect to get to school until the last of the week and maybe not then.

Main Street in Huntington was filled up for ten or fifteen feet. It was piled so high that all the principle stores on the north side of Main Street moved all of their goods to the second floor at the least sign of rain. When Main Street was dug out only narrow roads just wide enough for one way were dug. All the roads had to be dug out before they could be used. In some places they had to turn into lots and make the road run through them for a ways.

*Tired from hours of shoveling, a group of men stretch their muscles outside the Long Island Hotel in Hempstead, New York. (Hempstead Public Library)*

132

The trains are all blocked up. The one that started for New York from here last Monday morning has not got there yet and the one that left New York for here is a little more than half way here. The telegraph wires were all broken so that since one week ago yesterday only thirteen telegrams have been received in Huntington.

The [Long Island] Sound is of use now for one boat went to New York from here last week. When it came back, Saturday, it brought some of the mail and other things that were needed. It also took and brought passengers. This has been our only communication with New York for a week.

It was not until a week after the beginning of the storm that a small amount of mail reached Greenport, Long Island. The Long Island Railroad's tracks were still blocked, but the mail was delivered from New York to New London, Connecticut, and then ferried across Long Island Sound.

*This Long Island Railroad passenger train got stranded at Rockaway Junction, near Jamaica, New York. (Queens Library)*

*From the tower of this house in Hempstead, Long Island, historian Benjamin F. Thompson could survey the damage inflicted by the Blizzard of '88 on his home town. A man dressed only in shirtsleeves attempts to break a path with his horse in the foreground. (Hempstead Public Library)*

## The Storm That Changed America

*Reporters and editors worked throughout the storm inside this Hartford building to insure that* The Hartford Courant *continued its unblemished record of not missing a scheduled issue since its founding in 1764. Unlike some other Connecticut newspapers, the* Courant *published daily editions throughout the storm. Carriers were promised double pay if they completed their regular routes during the Blizzard. Enterprising hawkers sold papers that normally cost two cents to news-starved readers on the streets for as much as 50 cents. Today,* The Hartford Courant *is the oldest American newspaper in continuous publication. (Archives, History and Genealogy Unit, Connecticut State Library)*

A few years after the Great Storm, Charles Dudley Warner would write in the *Hartford Courant,* "Everybody talks about the weather, but nobody does anything about it." The statement struck the imagination of readers. In the folklore of quotations, it soon was attributed to another literary Hartfordite with the pen name of Mark Twain. Warner's expression may have captured the readers' minds but it wasn't entirely accurate. The Blizzard had profound effects on how America's cities prepared for disasters and how the urban infrastructure was developed.

In many cities the storm provided the stimulus for improvements in public transportation. Electrically powered streetcars were already on the scene in Richmond, Virginia, but the Blizzard gave the newly developed technology an added boost. Electric streetcars, it was discovered, also made snow removal easier. With an electric engine mounted on the car itself, plows could be pushed from the rear instead of the inefficient method of having a horse pull the plow over the snow. Electrically powered cars would soon prove more reliable and sturdier than horsedrawn vehicles, too. There were no worries about the survival of draft animals in the cold, and a cutoff of feed supplies would no longer force a suspension of schedules. Horsecars continued to ply Manhattan streets until 1916, but the Blizzard certainly hastened their demise.

The storm-related accident on the Third Avenue elevated led city planners to turn their thoughts underground for future mass transportation projects. New York needed reliable transportation for the million or more residents who now depended on it to get to work or around town. The Blizzard gave those New Yorkers who decried the elevated roads as eyesores anyhow a new weapon in the battle to prevent their construction. Calls for new elevated designs were soon met with loud cries to take the transit systems below street level. Although New Yorkers put up with towering ironwork above city streets and the cacophonous shriek of steel wheels against curved rails until the last elevated tracks were torn down in Manhattan almost 70 years later, the Blizzard of '88 provided the impetus for the development of subways throughout the city. The same calls for underground

*Oxen haul a wagon on a snow-clogged street near the State Capitol in Hartford. (Archives, History and Genealogy Unity, Connecticut State Library)*

*Onlookers at the South Norwalk, Connecticut, station gape at one of the first trains to resume a regular schedule after the Blizzard. Considering the almost complete paralysis of the rail system, many riders probably thought the trains would never move again. As it was, service was crippled on many lines for weeks after the storm as damage from derailments put locomotives out of service. (Wilton Historical Society)*

*Telegraph poles lean precariously, held up only by the strength of wires on the other side of the street in this New York scene. When wires touched, short circuits often resulted and made undamaged wires unusable. (The New York Historical Society)*

railways were heard by transportation planners in Boston and Philadelphia, too. Seven years later, Boston opened the first subway tunnel in North America carrying electrically powered street cars below Boston Common. New Yorkers took their first rides underground in 1904.

The total breakdown of communications forced a long and hard look at how America's cities were wired. With the proliferation of telegraph and telephone lines in the last half of the 19th century, city and town sidewalks had been festooned with totems holding as many as 100 different wires. Many poles snapped completely in the Blizzard's winds, crippling dozens of lines. Other lines shorted out when one wire broke loose and fell on those below it.

When the storm blacked out communications between Washington and the rest of the United States, congressmen and senators raised concern. Anarchy or foreign invaders might have swept the land during those dark hours; there was no way of knowing without the communications network that had been entrusted to precarious overhead lines. Incited by the storm's destruction, one senator was heard to assert: "We cannot control the elements. We cannot prevent another Blizzard. We can protect our communications. All wires now running overhead must be placed underground in urban areas and thus shielded from the caprices of nature. Not only are the overhead wires unsafe and unsightly — they are a damned menace to the security of the United States of America."

Telegraph and telephone companies began digging up pavement for underground cable conduits almost as soon as the snow was cleared. Within a few years, nearly all telegraph and telephone lines in urban areas were underground.

The Blizzard had at least a temporary impact on winter sports in Springfield, Massachusetts. Thrilled by the exploits of Moses A. Maillet, a French-Canadian immigrant who laughed at the Great Storm's fury by delivering newspapers on snowshoes during its height, several sports enthusiasts formed the Massassoit Snowshoe Club. The club disbanded after three years, however, because subsequent winters were not severe enough.

*Fashioned from saplings growing outside the windows of Session's Clock Factory in Forestville, Connecticut, and lashed together with cord used in the plant, these snowshoes allowed Frederick C. Stephenson of Plainville, Connecticut, to get home during the Blizzard of '88. Many workers in storm-affected areas used materials at hand to make snowshoes and keep themselves from sinking into the drifts as they walked home. (Plainville Historical Society)*

## Preserving The Memories

Along Old Stamford Road in New Canaan, Connecticut, a high drift formed during the storm, completely burying the telegraph wires that ran parallel to the road. The snow packed hard enough for adventurous children to walk along the ridge of the drift above the impacted lines. On Sunday, April 29, 1888, a day when temperatures reached 100°F in the sun, the snow there was still 14 inches deep. The memories of the Blizzard would last a lot longer.

In 1929 Theodorus Van Wyck, a writer living in Valley Stream, New York, and Thomas Gilleran, a New York lawyer, discussed their experiences during the Blizzard of '88 at a chance meeting in New York's City Hall. As they reminisced, they speculated on how many survivors were still living and agreed to try to get some of them together. That chance meeting was the beginning of the Blizzard Men and Ladies of 1888.

*Below and facing page: A comparison of Main Street in Hartford, Connecticut, before and after the Blizzard. (The Connecticut Historical Society)*

Soon after, Van Wyck placed a newspaper advertisement asking Blizzard veterans to contact Gilleran. Fourteen men responded and met on January 29, 1929, at Gilleran's office to exchange accounts about their Blizzard adventures. A month later, Van Wyck called another meeting. So many responded that Gilleran's office overflowed with Blizzard survivors. With a formal organization in place, the Blizzard Men decided to march to City Hall on the forty-first anniversary of the storm to meet with Mayor James J. Walker. Taken by the spirit of the event, Walker arranged for the Blizzard Men to be joined by polar explorer Sir Hubert Wilkins who happened to be visiting the city that day.

A second formal meeting convened March 12, 1930, and cemented the organization. By now, there were more than 100 dues-paying members. At the Machinery Club on New York's Church Street, those in attendance heard about the Blizzard exploits of 90-year-old Arthur Millbury and 75-year-old Eugene Todd. The group also decided to collect historical data on the storm and place it for safekeeping with the New York Historical Society. For more than seven years after that meeting, Dr. Samuel Meredith Strong gathered material from those who remembered the event, culminating in the publication of *The Great Blizzard of 1888* on the storm's fiftieth anniversary in 1938.

*The Blizzard Men of 1888 gather in the ballroom of New York City's Hotel Pennsylvania to celebrate the 50th anniversary of the Blizzard on March 12, 1938. (The New York Historical Society)*

Even as the ranks were thinned by the death of older members, the Blizzard Men and Ladies continued to meet annually through the 1960s to exchange tales and add storm-related memorabilia to the archives. "The Blizzard Men," a poem by Alice M. Sayer, dedicated to the survivors of the Great Blizzard of 1888 and printed in the 1963 annual meeting program, recalls the camaraderie of those who survived the icy blast:

Come, Blizzard Men of Eighty-eight,
 Let's gather 'round and mark the date,
The Twelfth of March so long ago,
 When the snow came down and the winds did blow.
The storm ne'er ceased for three whole days,
 The clouds hid all the sun's bright rays,
No trains could run, all wires down,
 No contacts made with any town.

We arose that morn to a dazzling sight,
 The snow was piled in mounds so white,
We wondered how we'd get to work,
 For we are the kind who do not shirk.
We'll tell you tales of ice and sleet,
 And drifts of snow across the street;
The greatest storm we'll ever know,
 Which came to us long ago.

May our dear Father lead the way,
 Protect and guide us day by day,
And in life's storms be ever near,
 And fill our hearts with hope and cheer.
May we all meet again next year,
 To greet the friends we hold so dear;
And once again we'll go our way,
 With memories of this happy day.

*By the end of the week it was business as usual for most retailers, including S. Silverthau & Sons jewelers in New Haven. (The Connecticut Historical Society)*

# Chapter 8— Notes On the Storm

In 1888, newspapers held a virtual monopoly on the mass media and advertising vehicles. Major cities boasted at least two or three publications in hot competition for readers, and every small town supported one daily. Priced at a few pennies, newspapers were available to all but the most impecunious readers. Telegraphic links brought dispatches from distant cities rapidly. With swift distribution possible through a broad network of railroad links and express train service between cities, out-of-town newspapers were often available to readers on a same day or next day schedule. Hardly any informed citizen would be caught without a daily ration of newsprint.

While the Blizzard managed to stop or slow down almost all working endeavors and professions, journalists stayed on the job bringing the news to readers. Reporters and editors working for morning editions were up against deadlines as the snowflakes fell on Sunday night and Monday morning. Sensing an impending story, many remained at their posts, digesting and writing the storm's history and its effect on people and places.

Reporting became more difficult when sinuous telegraph links broke down in the Blizzard's early hours. Most major newspapers were members of the Associated Press and shared reports by telegraph transmission. As lines between cities snapped and communications were broken, dozens of alternative routes were designed. New York newspapers, cut off from Washington, got stories from the nation's capital via Chicago and Cincinnati. In storm-tossed Manchester, New Hampshire, for example, news from Boston made a roundabout journey through Montreal. The only way for telegraphers in Boston to reach New York was through the trans-Atlantic cable to London, a round trip distance of 6,000 miles. The remaining links were taxed to the limits as more and more messages were detoured.

Lacking the machinery of the Associated Press and other news-gathering organizations, local reporters and editors were forced to return to the techniques of 50 years earlier to obtain stories. Editors began to appreciate the long-winded contributors who usually badgered them with prodigious stories in quieter times. As a result, few details were ignored or overlooked

*Yale upperclassmen pose for the photographer while sitting on the cowcatcher of a New York, New Haven & Hartford locomotive outside the New Haven depot. (New Haven Colony Historical Society)*

in local reports of the storm and the tragedy that accompanied it. These contemporary reports provide a comprehensive look at the lives of people who lived through the Blizzard of '88 and how they managed the situation.

The journalists of 1888 etched the Blizzard in the minds of those who lived through it and preserved its memory for later generations. The four- and eight-page editions, crammed with Blizzard news set in six point type, are a monument to their inventiveness and dedication. The reports filed with city editors, set by a typographer on a newly invented Linotype machine, matted and cast in lead for the steam-powered rotary press, and delivered to homes or hawked on the streets by ambitious newsboys provide a complete picture of the Blizzard and the way people coped with its effects.

## *The Other Blizzard of 1888*

Although the storm that struck the northeastern states from March 11 to March 14, 1888, is commonly known as "The Blizzard of '88," midwesterners remember another meteorological event under the same name.

Between January 12 and 14, 1888, what was then the West—from Montana and the Dakotas South to Texas and East to Wisconsin, and the prairie provinces of Canada suffered through raging snow, winds gusting to 60 miles per hour, and temperatures as low as -52°F. In its three-day reign, this blizzard killed 237 persons, a phenomenally high figure for such a thinly populated area, and tens of thousands of cattle and other livestock. Trains were stuck in the open prairies for as long as three days. The high winds blew down grain elevators scattering thousands of tons of stored wheat and grain over the countryside.

Railroads serving the midwest had one distinct advantage in fighting this storm. Unlike their eastern counterparts, the midwestern rail companies had quickly adopted new technology for snow removal using rotary snow plows. With massive augers to chew through the drifts, the rotary plows made short work of most drifts. Along one stretch of track in the Dakotas, locomotives using the new equipment were able to clear a 200-mile stretch of track in just 16 hours after the snowfall stopped.

# Three Centuries of Memorable Snowstorms

Chronology of major snowstorms along the northeastern coast of the United States from the late seventeenth to the twentieth century.

### Jan. 4–Feb. 23, 1698. "The Terriblest Winter."

Journal of John Pike of Dover, NH, reported 17 days of snow during this period. Toward the end of February the records of the First Church of Christ in Cambridge, MA, reported 42″ on the ground in Cambridge.

### Feb. 27–Mar. 7, 1717. "The Great Snow of 1717."

Actually four snowstorms bunched together that hit a wide region of New England in succession, leaving 3 feet in Boston and up to 5 feet elsewhere, with drifts exceeding 25 feet. Referred to as "The Great Snow" more than one hundred years later.

### Mar. 24, 1765.

This storm followed a track from Pennsylvania to Massachusetts, dropping snow up to two and one half feet or more on the level.

### Jan. 27–28, 1772. "The Washington and Jefferson Snowstorm."

Named thus because the storm marooned George Washington in Mount Vernon and Thomas Jefferson in Monticello. Snowfall was estimated at three feet on a level across Virginia and Maryland.

### Dec. 26, 1778. "The Hessian Storm."

A severe blizzard with high winds and bitter cold that occurred during the Revolutionary War. The storm covered a swath from Pennsylvania to southern New England. Rhode Island, which was occupied by Hessian soldiers, was hit hardest with drifts up to 16½ feet.

### Jan. 26–28, 1805.

This storm dumped heavy snows on New York City and New England. Snow fell steadily for 48 hours in New York City, which reported over two feet.

### Jan. 14–16, 1831. "The Great Snowstorm."

This storm produced heavy snowfall over a large area from the Ohio Valley to the eastern seaboard north of Georgia, with 30″ and more from Pennsylvania across southern New England.

*Jan. 8–10, 1836.*

Became known as "The Big Snow" for New York, northern Pennsylvania, and western New England, where two to three feet fell.

*Mar. 11–14, 1888. "The Blizzard of '88."*

The most legendary of all historic snowstorms in the Northeast. Blizzard conditions lasted for two to three days across Pennsylvania, New Jersey, New York, and western and southern New England, where depths of three to four feet were predominant.

*Mar. 27, 1898. "Portland Storm."*

Passenger ship Portland sunk off Cape Cod in hurricane-force winds and all 200 on board died. Twenty-seven inches of snow fell at New London, CT.

*Feb. 12–14, 1899. "The Blizzard of '99."*

Characterized by one of the coldest periods ever experienced in the eastern United States. Snow fell from central Florida up to Maine with Washington, DC, getting 20½" and Cape May, NJ, getting 34".

*Jan. 27–29, 1922. "The Knickerbocker Storm."*

Oddly it occurred on the 150th anniversary of the "Washington and Jefferson" storm. Snow fell heaviest in Virginia and Maryland with 28" in Washington, DC, caving in the roof of the Knickerbocker Theatre and killing 100 people.

*Feb. 19–20, 1934.*

This blizzard walloped southern New England during the coldest February on record. Twenty-two inches of snow fell at Bridgeport and New Haven, CT.

*Dec. 26–27, 1947.*

A surprise snowstorm produced the heaviest 24-hour accumulation of snow in New York City's modern records with 26.4" and 32" in the suburbs, most of which fell within a twelve-hour period.

*Mar. 2–5, 1960.*

This was a widespread late winter storm that turned especially fierce in eastern New England where 20" to 30" of snow fell with near hurricane force winds. Nantucket's snowfall measured 31.3", Blue Hill Observatory, 30.3" and Boston, 19.8".

### Jan. 19–20, 1961. "The Kennedy Inaugural Storm."

This storm was the second big storm of the winter and occurred on the eve of John F. Kennedy's inauguration in Washington where 8″ of snow fell. Ten to 20″ fell over the Northeast, the same as the previous storm, with 10″ in New York, 12″ in Boston and 13″ in Philadelphia.

### Jan. 29–31, 1966. "The Blizzard of '66."

This storm combined with "lake-effect" snowfall off Lake Ontario produced extreme depths of 30″ to 60″ or greater across portions of New York State. Washington, DC, measured 20″ with high winds and temperatures in the teens. The storm was the last in the series of three snowstorms to affect the Middle Atlantic states over a one-week period.

### Feb. 24–28, 1969.

Produced some of the heaviest snowfall on record across eastern New England with 30″ or more from eastern Massachusetts and New Hampshire into much of central Maine. Twenty-six inches fell at Boston where it snowed for 100 straight hours, but the heaviest snows fell in the mountainous areas of New Hampshire and Maine with 77″ at Pinkham Notch at the base of Mt. Washington. The following snow depths were recorded: Rockport, MA, 39″, Portsmouth, NH, 34″, Portland, ME, 27″ and Old Town, ME, 44″.

### Feb. 6–7, 1978. "The Great Wind and Snow Storm of '78."

Perhaps the worst snowstorm on record (in modern times) to hit southern and eastern New England, where 25″ to 40″ of snow was accompanied by winds gusting to near 100 mph. Schools and commerce were shut down from New York City and Long Island to eastern New England for a week or more. Thirty-eight inches fell in Woonsocket, RI, 28.6″ in Providence, RI, 27.1″ in Boston and 17.7″ in New York City.

### Feb. 10–12, 1983. "The So-Called Megalopolitan Storm."

Twenty or more inches fell in Washington, Baltimore, Philadelphia, and New York, one of the greatest snowfalls on record. Snow amounts were: Philadelphia, 21.3″, Harrisburg, 25″, Allentown, PA, 25.2″ and Hartford, CT, 21″.

# FRANK LESLIE'S
## ILLUSTRATED
## ·BLIZZARD·
## NEWSPAPER

Entered according to Act of Congress, in the year 1888, by Mrs. Frank Leslie, in the Office of the Librarian of Congress at Washington.— Entered at the Post Office, New York, N. Y., as Second-class Matter.

No. 1,697.—VOL. LXVI.]        NEW YORK—FOR THE WEEK ENDING MARCH 24, 1888.        [PRICE, 10 CENTS. $4.00 YEARLY. 13 WEEKS, $1.00.

THE GREAT STORM OF MARCH 12TH–13TH.—SCENE IN PRINTING-HOUSE SQUARE, NEW YORK CITY, SHOWING
THE TERRIBLE FORCE OF THE BLIZZARD.
FROM A SKETCH BY A STAFF ARTIST.—SEE PAGE 35.

# Chapter 9— Remembering the Great Storm

Although photography was close to its golden anniversary in 1888, few recognized the impact this evolving technology would have on how persons remembered the storm. Along with shovel-wielding laborers who cleared the streets, hundreds of photographers lugged bulky wooden cameras and cumbersome tripods to record the event.

Photography then was a far cry from today's point-and-shoot cameras. It meant preparing your own glass plate negatives, spending time crouched under a black hood at the back of a camera while setting up the shot and then later mixing the processing chemistry in the kitchen sink. You will notice that some photographs in this book are devoid of people and moving objects, or that they appear only as blurs. This is testimony to lengthy exposures in cold winter winds that were required to record such images.

Author Samuel Clemens, who was trapped in New York City and watched the Blizzard come and go through the windows of a suite at the Murray Hill Hotel, once said, "Get your facts first, then you can distort them as much as you please." Without evidence provided by amateur and professional photographers, the facts about the Blizzard would have been distorted into folklore. The drifts would have grown taller and the snow deeper as stories passed from grandfather to grandchild. The American folk tradition would have quickly absorbed the Blizzard, placing it next to Paul Bunyan and Pecos Bill.

For those who survived the Blizzard, a photograph of the storm served as a souvenir of a time when the entire community gathered to battle a common disaster. Decades later, it would still be the starting point of conversations. In the next 90 pages, you will be a part of the Blizzard era, perhaps in your own home town, thanks to those who took photographs and preserved them in tattered scrapbooks and historical society vaults.

*An old wives' tale probably harmed more frostbite sufferers than it helped. Snow rubbed on the affected extremities was a common remedy for frostbite. Here, a New York City police officer attempts to aid the exposed ears of one victim. Another salve of dubious medicinal value — molasses — was also touted as a frostbite cure. (Connecticut State Library)*

*Ice coats the sails of this wreck in Lewes Harbor, Delaware. (Connecticut State Library)*

*This engine left the tracks while trying to blaze a trail through the drifts near Flemington, New Jersey. (The New York Historical Society)*

*Tall snow drifts block a major intersection in Newark, New Jersey. (The New Jersey Historical Society)*

*Snow drifted high over the steps leading to these townhouses near the corner of High and Court Streets in Newark, New Jersey. In many areas, snow drifts would tower on one side of the street while the other side would remain almost bare. (The New Jersey Historical Society)*

150

A four-horse sleigh is one of the few vehicles on Market Street in Newark, New Jersey, in the hours following the storm. (The New Jersey Historical Society)

A lonely shoveler and a man on horseback are the only persons venturing into the snow on Front Street in Plainfield, New Jersey, just after the Blizzard. (The New York Historical Society)

Shovelful by shovelful, men and women nibbled away at drifts blocking sidewalks and streets throughout the Northeast. Rubbing his hands for warmth, this unidentified man dug out a passage on North Pearl Street in Albany, New York. (Albany Institute of History and Art)

The Blizzard's cold snap froze the waters of New York Bay. This photograph was taken four days after the storm. (Museum of the City of New York)

The wind-driven snow blotted out signs and coated almost everything with its sticky residue. (Albany Institute of History and Art)

The ice on New York Bay was thick enough to permit these two gentlemen to walk on the water on the day following the Blizzard. The New York and Sea Beach Railroad Dock appears in the background. (Museum of the City of New York)

*A wrecked pilot boat washed ashore near 72nd Street in the Bay Ridge section of Brooklyn. (Museum of the City of New York)*

*Three days after the Blizzard, crews shovel out the horsecar tracks on Flatbush Avenue. The storm had completely isolated the village of Flatbush from the rest of Brooklyn. The photograph was taken near Prospect Park. (Brooklyn Historical Society)*

On Monroe Place in Brooklyn, the heads of men digging out the sidewalk on the right side of the photograph are barely visible above the mounds of snow, while the opposite sidewalk is almost bare. The scene was repeated throughout the city. (Brooklyn Historical Society)

Parishioners could barely find the entrance to Plymouth Church in Brooklyn Heights, New York. (Brooklyn Historical Society)

155

With edges scalloped by the wind, this moderate drift on Brooklyn's Clark Street suggests an alpine arete. The cylindrical structure behind the drift is a telephone for emergency use by police. (Brooklyn Historical Society)

The city of Brooklyn paid $20,000 to a contractor to clear the snow under the elevated tracks along Fulton Street. (The Library of Congress)

*Little business was transacted by shopkeepers along Main Street in Hempstead, New York, in the hours after the Blizzard. (Hempstead Public Library)*

*Snow was piled high in front of Willets' Drug Store in Hempstead, New York. (Hempstead Public Library)*

*Snow still sticks to the trees after the Blizzard in Hempstead, New York. (Hempstead Public Library)*

*Several well-dressed gents survey the scene in front of the Occidental Hotel in Hempstead, New York. (Hempstead Public Library)*

George Hewmann's Lager Beer Saloon (left) probably sent patrons home dry during the Blizzard. Wagons from local breweries couldn't get through the snow-clogged streets and rum shop owners depended on daily deliveries to keep the inventory fresh. Geo. W. Conklin's establishment next door did better. A sign above the door advertises plows. The scene is Main Street and New York Avenue in Huntington, New York. (Huntington Historical Society)

The man standing on the snow bank at left is Dan Beard, founder of the Boy Scouts of America. The photograph was taken at the corner of Madison Avenue and Union Street in Jamaica, New York. (Queens Library)

A passing sleigh on Jamaica Ave. in Jamaica, New York. (Queens Library)

Stores along Jamaica Ave. in Jamaica, New York, are hidden by mounds of snow after the Blizzard. (Queens Library)

Anyone wanting to pay taxes or see the mayor in Jamaica, New York, had to first climb this drift. The large Victorian building is the town hall. (Queens Library)

Traffic on the Long Island Railroad near Jamaica, New York, stood still for several days following the Blizzard. (Queens Library)

*These two shovelers sank up to their thighs when they tried to walk across a snow drift on Union Avenue in Jamaica, New York. (Queens Library)*

*This fish market in Jamaica, New York, was temporarily put out of business by the Blizzard. Because fishing fleets did not go out during the storm and damage to boats hindered their ability to go to sea when skies finally cleared, seafood was in extremely short supply. (Queens Library)*

*Looking west along Fulton Street in Jamaica, New York. (Queens Library)*

*Tall snow drifts almost reach up to the electric power lines suspended above the middle of Fulton Street in Jamaica, New York. (Queens Library)*

More than one New Yorker wished he could be in the sunshine down south during and after the Blizzard. On Liberty Street, one woeful resident posted a sign declaring "This street closed. Oh! for Florida. Cut rates." (The New York Historical Society)

For those in need of directions after the Blizzard, one New York City wag planted a sign reading "This way to Canada" on a massive mound of snow on 14th Street. (The New York Historical Society)

*Flowers mark the burial site of Madison Square Park in New York City. The sign reads "The Flowers That Bloom In The Snow Ha Ha." (The New York Historical Society)*

*An abandoned horsecar sits blocked by snow in front of the Hotel Martin on University Place in lower Manhattan. (The New York Historical Society)*

*Along Woodbine Street in Brooklyn, Breading G. Way and his family marvel at the mounds of snow that accumulated during the storm. (The New York Historical Society*

# THE GREAT BLIZZARD OF TWENTY YEARS AGO
### Memorable Storm of March 12, 1888, Still Fresh in the Minds of New Yorkers

UNION SQUARE WITH THE THIRD DAY'S SNOWFALL

THE TROUBLES OF THE RAILROAD MEN

*Even 20 years later, New Yorkers were still talking about the Blizzard. This newspaper clipping is from the March 14, 1908 Saturday Evening Mail. (The New York Historical Society)*

*Workers attempt to remove a telegraph pole on West 11th Street in Manhattan that toppled into a garret window. (Museum of the City of New York)*

*Not much activity was going on in these offices on New York's Exchange Court. The mounds of snow in the courtyard blocked the entrance. (Museum of the City of New York)*

167

*Deep snows blocked this street in Northport, New York. The thoroughfare led to the harbor on Long Island Sound where many ships were wrecked during the Blizzard. (Northport Historical Society)*

*A view of snow-clogged Main Street in Ossining, New York. (Ossining Historical Society)*

Crews begin the arduous task of clearing the
snow by hand on Poughkeepsie's Main Street.
(Dutchess County Historical Society)

An archway sculptured in a Poughkeepsie,
New York, drift suggests Gothic architecture.
(Dutchess County Historical Society)

170

The spats worn by the derby-hatted gent at right offered little protection against wet feet in the Blizzard's snow. Taken on Tuesday, March 13, this photograph shows a drift blocking Catherine Street at the corner of Main Street in Poughkeepsie, New York. (Dutchess County Historical Society)

The scene on March 14, 1888, at the Hayt & Lindley Store, corner of Main and Garden Streets in Poughkeepsie, New York. (Dutchess County Historical Society)

*A mountain range of snow fills Main Street in Poughkeepsie, New York. (Dutchess County Historical Society)*

*Main Street in Poughkeepsie, New York, is completely blockaded to all wheeled traffic. Citizens caught without boots during the Blizzard probably made the "Rubber Sale" at S. B. Thing & Co.'s store (at left) a great success. (Dutchess County Historical Society)*

*A shoveler clears the last traces of ice and hard packed snow from a sidewalk in front of a Poughkeepsie, New York, store. (Dutchess County Historical Society)*

*Snow is piled as high as a horse's head in this stereopticon view taken in Matteawan, New York. (Dutchess County Historical Society)*

*Three aristocratic looking gents wield shovels atop a drift in Saratoga Springs, New York. (Collection of George S. Bolster)*

*The trunks of tall elms in front of the Grand Union Hotel in Saratoga Springs, New York, are completely covered by mounds of snow. This upstate city received some of the deepest snow in the entire Blizzard area. (Historical Society of Saratoga Springs)*

174

A man standing on top of a massive snow drift in front of the American and Adelphi hotels in Saratoga Springs towers over his friends on the sidewalk below. (Historical Society of Saratoga Springs)

A hollow dug in a giant snow drift on Broadway in Saratoga Springs, New York, suggests an igloo. (Historical Society of Saratoga Springs)

*High drifts greeted guests at the United States Hotel in Saratoga Springs. (Collection of George S. Bolster)*

*The view through the snow arch on Broadway looking down towards Phila Street in Saratoga Springs, New York. (Historical Society of Saratoga Springs)*

*Saratoga Springs residents pictured on the sidewalk are probably wondering if the lofty piles of snow will melt before the summer tourist season begins. (Historical Society of Saratoga Springs)*

Snow in the middle of First Street in Troy, New York, is left untouched after the storm cleared. The street was known as "Bankers Row" because of the proliferation of financial firms and brokerage houses. The snowbanks, however, were the only ones here doing a brisk business. (Rensselaer County Historical Society)

Residents of the neighborhood near First and Congress Streets in Troy, New York, crowd around the snow drifts. (Rensselaer County Historical Society)

There were plenty of deposits in the "snow banks" on the sidewalk in front of Troy Savings Bank in Troy, New York. (Rensselaer County Historical Society)

Untouched snow drifts in a Troy, New York, alleyway tower over a resident. (Rensselaer County Historical Society)

A narrow walkway carved in the snow for pedestrians was the only way to get home in this residential neighborhood in Troy, New York. Fifty-five inches of snow buried this Hudson River city. (Rensselaer County Historical Society)

Down to the tracks at last! Second Avenue in Lansingburgh (now a part of Troy), New York, is finally clear enough to operate horsecars. The large sign suspended above the street is transparent and seen from the rear, which explains the reversed lettering. (Rensselaer County Historical Society)

*A reporter for the Naugatuck Valley Sentinel peers at the snow from a second floor window in Ansonia, Connecticut (Old Derby Historical Society)*

*Enormous drifts of snow block display windows of stores in Ansonia, Connecticut. (Old Derby Historical Society)*

*Main Street in Ansonia, Connecticut, is piled high with snow following the Blizzard. Note the early electric street lights suspended above the street. The large brick building in the center of the photograph is Ansonia's Opera House. (Old Derby Historical Society)*

*Employees of the Bullard Machine Company assume a victorious pose atop a pile of snow cleared from the entrance of their shop in Bridgeport, Connecticut. (Bridgeport Public Library)*

*Workers at the corner of State and Main Streets in Bridgeport load a horsedrawn dump wagon with snow. (The Connecticut Historical Society)*

*A child's imagination could run wild in the mountains of snow blocking Cannon Street in Bridgeport, Connecticut. The nooks and crannies in the drifts provided plenty of hiding places during the snowball fights that ensued in the days after the blizzard. (The Connecticut Historical Society)*

A homeowner takes a break for the photographer while clearing a path on Bridgeport's Liberty Street. (Bridgeport Public Library)

Tall mounds of snow surround the Hub Clothing House at the corner of State and Main Streets in Bridgeport. (Bridgeport Public Library)

184

*Engine No. 100 couldn't navigate through this drift at the Emmett Street grade crossing in Bristol, Connecticut. One young lad who loaded up with a pile of hot-off-the-press newspapers trudged eight hours to reach a snowbound train such as this and reaped a harvest selling two-cent copies for one dollar to customers eager for news. (Bristol Historical Society)*

*What looks like a ski area's bunny slope is actually Main Street in Bristol, Connecticut. A young boy strikes a jaunty pose while, at left, someone who was sweeping the last of the snow from a sidewalk ducks into an entryway. (Bristol Historical Society)*

A tall snow drift blocks the side door of this
Danbury, Connecticut, home. (The Connecticut Historical Society)

Grocer George Gardner (at right) of Danbury, Connecticut, waits for customers outside his Main Street store the day after the
Blizzard.(The Connecticut Historical Society)

Milk, bread, cakes and pies were scarce commodities after the Blizzard in some communities, but not at the market on Main Street in Derby, Connecticut. A banner hanging over the sidewalk at the left side of this photograph advertises their availability. The boy standing atop the snow piled in the middle of the street looks like he is ready to toss a snowball at the photographer. (Derby Public Library)

Photographers often enhanced scenes of the blizzard to make an image look as if it was taken during the height of the storm. Fake snow created on the negative by a deft hand and paint brush adds to the romance of this scene shot in Derby, Connecticut. (Derby Public Library)

Snow banks six feet high remained after the sidewalk was cleared in front of the Moran Brush Manufacturing Company in Hamden, Connecticut. (New Haven Colony Historical Society)

A deep canyon through a snow drift in Fairfield, Connecticut. (Fairfield County Historical Society)

A pencil sketch by Eliza Butler McCook depicts the drifts that clogged Main Street in Hartford, Connecticut. McCook only had to look out her living room window to see the devastation wrought by the storm. (The Antiquarian and Landmarks Society)

Two well-dressed chaps survey a snow-filled scene in Hartford, Connecticut. (The Connecticut Historical Society)

Hartford's City Hall, a building erected by Charles Bulfinch almost 100 years earlier to serve as the State House, looms over the shoulders of a trio of shovelers. (Archives, History and Genealogy Unit, Connecticut State Library)

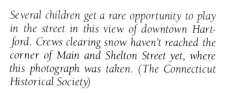

Several children get a rare opportunity to play in the street in this view of downtown Hartford. Crews clearing snow haven't reached the corner of Main and Shelton Street yet, where this photograph was taken. (The Connecticut Historical Society)

*Hartford's Asylum Street was almost impassable before shoveling crews cleared the sidewalks. Only a few footprints indicate where brave souls attempted to tread in the deep snow. (Archives, History and Genealogy Unit, Connecticut State Library)*

*Two children peered at photographer E. P. Kellogg through this deep cut in the snow banks along Hartford's Main Street. The Pratt & Sage store is still in business in Hartford 100 years later as Sage-Allen. (Archives, History and Genealogy Unit, Connecticut State Library)*

Hartford's Kinsley Street is completely closed in by snow. (The Connecticut Historical Society)

A solid wall of snow and a cast iron fence forced pedestrians to walk single file on this Grove Street sidewalk in Hartford, Connecticut. (The Connecticut Historical Society)

Hartford's busiest intersection, Main and State Streets, was filled with snow piled higher than the average man or woman's head. (The Connecticut Historical Society)

Dozens of telegraph lines sweep over the sidewalk and street from the office of the United Lines Telegraph Company on Hartford's Central Row. The storm hastened the removal of overhead lines to underground conduits. (The Connecticut Historical Society)

*Local residents of Hartford's Clinton Street pose for the photographer. The top of a tunnel through the drift is visible at right. (The Connecticut Historical Society)*

*Art lovers who wanted to visit America's oldest public art museum, The Wadsworth Atheneum (the castle-like structure at the end of the street) first had to deal with this mound of snow on Mulberry Street in Hartford. (The Connecticut Historical Society)*

A young boy is the only person in sight at the intersection of Main and State Streets in Hartford. On a normal day, this would be the busiest corner in town, crowded with wagons, streetcars and pedestrians. (The Connecticut Historical Society)

Massive snow drifts block the intersection of Pearl and Main Streets in Hartford (Archives, History and Genealogy Unit, Connecticut State Library)

Shoppers were undaunted by the drifts in downtown Hartford as this photograph of Asylum Street taken two days after the storm suggests. The hand-lettered sign stuck in the snow bank at right advertises spring overcoats. (*The Connecticut Historical Society*)

A photographer catches his competition in Manchester, Connecticut. Just behind and slightly to the left of the dog, another photographer adjusts his focus beneath the hood of a view camera mounted on a tripod. The shot was taken on North Main Street near the intersection of North School Street in front of the Allen House. (Connecticut National Bank, North Manchester Branch)

Perhaps anticipating that graffiti artists might destroy the aesthetics of this tunnel through a snow drift in Meriden, Connecticut, the "architect" placed a sign reading "Please Not Deface This Tunnel" above the entrance. (Meriden Historical Society)

*A sweeping view of Meriden, Connecticut, after the Blizzard from City Hall's steps. (Meriden Historical Society)*

*With drifts towering above their heads, men, women and children pose for the photographer on Colony Street in Meriden, Connecticut. (Meriden Historical Society)*

*The sculpturing effect of wind on snow gave a streamlined look to this locomotive at the Meriden, Connecticut, depot. After crashing into a track-blocking drift, the snow stuck on the engine's cowcatcher. (Meriden Historical Society)*

*Digging out Cooley's Livery Stable on West Main Street in Meriden, Connecticut. (Meriden Historical Society)*

*J. Howard Thompson (standing) stops to chat about the weather with G. Ellsworth Meech (on horseback) on the streets of Middletown, Connecticut. (Middlesex County Historical Society)*

Long icicles hang from the gutters of the Meriden House in Meriden, Connecticut. High drifts prevent passers-by from seeing the new spring fashions that were probably displayed in the windows of the clothing store located on the first floor. (Meriden Historical Society)

Snow was piled to eye level in Middletown, Connecticut. (Middlesex County Historical Society)

A team of eight oxen drag a sled through snow-covered streets in Middletown, Connecticut. (Middlesex County Historical Society)

Tall snow banks hem in a bare sidewalk in Middletown, Connecticut (Middlesex County Historical Society)

These two men almost seem to be guarding the snow on Main Street in Middletown, Connecticut. The busy Connecticut River town was brought to its knees by 50 inches of snow, the greatest amount ever to fall during a single snowstorm in Connecticut. (Middlesex County Historical Society)

Stereopticon cards were popular artifacts of the Blizzard. This one depicts State Street in New Haven, Connecticut. (New Haven Colony Historical Society)

Mounds of snow stacked next to the sidewalk dwarf a child on Church Street in New Haven. (New Haven Colony Historical Society)

Children play near two horsecars stalled side by side on Whalley Avenue in New Haven. (New Haven Colony Historical Society)

*Patrons of the People's Theatre in New Haven had an arduous climb over a mountain of snow to reach the box office. (New Haven Colony Historical Society)*

*Snow drifts almost completely cover first-floor windows at the Yale University School of Art (New Haven Colony Historical Society)*

Tall banks of snow hide a cast iron fence near a wheel shop on New Haven's York Street. (New Haven Colony Historical Society)

Clearing the sidewalk in front of the main post office on Church Street in New Haven, Connecticut. (New Haven Colony Historical Society)

Snow removed from New Haven's streets was unloaded on the New Haven Green to melt. (New Haven Colony Historical Society)

Mounds of snow block the view of businesses along Orange Street in New Haven, Connecticut. (New Haven Colony Historical Society)

*A solitary wagon passes by two abandoned horsecars near the New Haven Green. (New Haven Colony Historical Society)*

*Only a few pedestrians ventured on normally busy Chapel Street in New Haven, Connecticut, after the Blizzard. (New Haven Colony Historical Society)*

*Slush fills New Haven's Church Street a few days after the Blizzard. (New Haven Colony Historical Society)*

*Snow-covered New Haven Green. (New Haven Colony Historical Society)*

*Even a horse has a hard time seeing over this pile of snow on Elm Street in Rockville, Connecticut. (Vernon Historical Society)*

*Stately homes in Rockville, Connecticut, are barricaded by snow. (Vernon Historical Society)*

*Union Street in Rockville, Connecticut, is impassable the day after the Blizzard. Three weeks after this photograph was taken, the entire block including the Second Congregational Church was destroyed by fire. (Vernon Historical Society)*

*Two men sample the crisp winter air aboard a horsedrawn sled in Rockville, Connecticut. (Vernon Historical Society)*

Passengers await the arrival of the first trains at the South Norwalk station after the Blizzard. At right, shovelers attempt to clear a sidewalk blocked by a drift that almost reached the top of the street lamps. (Wilton Historical Society)

Piles of cleared snow dwarf a laborer working on a railroad right of way near South Norwalk, Connecticut.(Darien Historical Society)

*A one-horse open sleigh with a bare-headed driver traverses the lonely streets of Norwalk, Connecticut, immediately following the Blizzard (Wilton Historical Society)*

*A track clearing crew for the New York, New Haven & Hartford Railroad pauses for the photographer in the snow-clogged Highland Avenue cut in Norwalk, Connecticut. (Darien Historical Society)*

*This overhanging roof did little to keep the snow off the sidewalk at the corner of High and Main Streets in Southington, Connecticut. (Barnes Museum, Southington)*

*Snow almost reaches above the horses' backs as a wagon travels down North Main Street in Southington, Connecticut. (Barnes Museum, Southington)*

*Three unidentified men stand on drifted snow next to railroad tracks in Stratford, Connecticut. The snow was often very deep in places where tracks ran in open cuts below grade level. (Bridgeport Public Library)*

*Look carefully at the center of this photograph. You'll note a person shoveling snow from the roof of this elaborate home in Waterbury, Connecticut. (Torrington Historical Society)*

*Persons who wanted to visit the Waterbury One Price Store for its clearance sale had to wait until clearance of the snow on the sidewalk was complete. (The Connecticut Historical Society)*

ADT & BROTHER, PHOTOGRAPHERS,                    48 AND 63 BANK ST., WATERBURY,

AFTER THE GREAT BLIZZARD,

*Few trains arrived or departed from the Waterbury, Connecticut, depot until snow was cleared from the tracks. (Torrington Historical Society)*

216

*Drifted snow clogs Exchange Place in Waterbury, Connecticut. (The Connecticut Historical Society)*

*Waterbury, Connecticut's schools closed for an entire week, giving an unexpected vacation to these children. One camera-shy girl refused to join the group in this portrait. (Torrington Historical Society)*

*Clearing the roads in the countryside of western Connecticut was no easy matter. (Torrington Historical Society)*

*Enormous drifts blocked the front doors of these Waterbury, Connecticut, homes. (Torrington Historical Society)*

*Tall mounds of snow blocked the view of retail shop windows on this Waterbury, Connecticut, street. (Torrington Historical Society)*

*A long blanket overcoat and a knit stocking cap protect this horseback rider from the cold on the streets of Greenfield, Massachusetts. (Historical Society of Greenfield)*

Workers clear the last vestiges of the storm from the sidewalk outside the Mansion House Hotel in Greenfield, Massachusetts. (Historical Society of Greenfield)

Some very precise shoveling created this vertical wall of snow on Main Street in Greenfield, Massachusetts. (Historical Society of Greenfield)

*We did it! A snow shovel brigade pauses for a victory photo beside a conquered drift in Greenfield, Massachusetts. (Historical Society of Greenfield)*

*This narrow tunnel allowed pedestrians to cross Main Street in Northampton, Massachusetts. (The New York Historical Society)*

221

Tunnels were in vogue along the streets of Northampton, Massachusetts. Four merchants dug through the drifts to allow access to their Main Street stores. (Northampton Historical Society)

M.M. French & Co. dug this cut through the drifts clogging Northampton's Main Street to help customers get to their store. (Northampton Historical Society)

A narrow tunnel pierces a drift on Main Street in Northampton, Massachusetts. (Northampton Historical Society)

Deep drifts reach above the tops of first floor windows along Main Street in Northampton, Massachusetts, while the opposite side of the street is swept almost bare by the wind. (Northampton Historical Society)

*A lad wields a shovel in Northampton, Massachusetts. (Northampton, Historical Society)*

*Edward's Dining Room in Northampton, Massachusetts welcomes patrons by clearing the sidewalk in front of the establishment. (Northampton Historical Society)*

A lone shoveler challenges drifted snow as high as his head on North Street in Pittsfield, Massachusetts. (Berkshire County Historical Society)

Piles of snow completely cover first-floor store windows on North Street in Pittsfield, Massachusetts. (Berkshire County Historical Society)

Park Square in Pittsfield, Massachusetts.
(Berkshire County Historical Society)

Signs atop snow drifts advertise a piano
dealer in Pittsfield, Massachusetts. The old
Academy of Music building is across the
street. (Berkshire County Historical Society)

Shovelers fill a horsedrawn sled with snow on Main Street in Springfield, Massachusetts. (Springfield Public Library)

An abandoned horsecar is stranded by snow in the middle of Main Street in Springfield, Massachusetts. (The New York Historical Society)

An engine half hidden by drifted snow emerges from the Springfield, Massachusetts, depot. (Springfield Public Library)

Two dapper fellows stride down Springfield's Main Street while a horsedrawn wagon struggled through the snow in the street. (Springfield Public Library)

"Why me?" the man with upraised arms seems to be asking. The question undoubtedly crossed the minds of thousands of people who endured the hardships presented by the Blizzard of '88. This photograph was taken on Main Street in Springfield, Massachusetts, a day or two after the storm. (Springfield Public Library)

The shell of the former Springfield Union newspaper building stands forlorn after the Blizzard. A fire devastated the five-story structure on March 7, 1888. (Springfield Public Library)

Hard work resulted in this bare brick sidewalk on John Street in Worcester, Massachusetts. (American Antiquarian Society)

Snow-laden trees are weighed down in front of these row houses on Elm Street in Worcester, Massachusetts. (American Antiquarian Society)

*No one was walking through the Square in Bellows Falls, Vermont after the Blizzard. (Rockingham Public Library)*

*James Grandy (with shovel) assists in track clearing at the Brattleboro depot. The southbound train at the station platform got stalled here on Monday noon and didn't continue its journey until Thursday morning. (Brattleboro P.H.O.T.O.S.)*

The ice cream parlor on Elliot Street in Brattleboro, Vermont, probably had few customers in the days following the Blizzard. (Brattleboro P.H.O.T.O.S.)

For many years, this wind gauge atop Mount Wantastiquet was an item of conversation for residents of Brattleboro, Vermont. The direction and velocity readings were transmitted by wire to Randall & Clapp's Jewelry Store on Main Street. At right, A. E. Randall (left) and Ferris Vaughan make a minor adjustment on the recording mechanism. (Brattleboro P.H.O.T.O.S.)

*Deep snow blocks Main Street in Brattleboro, Vermont. (Brattleboro P.H.O.T.O.S.)*

*Snow drifted almost up to the porch roof on these stately homes in Brattleboro, Vermont. (Brattleboro P.H.O.T.O.S.)*

In Brattleboro, Vermont, the Baptists poured out of the church on the left and the Congregationalists exited the church on the right on Sunday, March 11, 1888, not knowing that the street would be filled with waist-deep snow just 48 hours later. (Brattleboro P.H.O.T.O.S.)

While most Vermonters could only grind their teeth in anger about the storm, E. Crosey & Co. in Brattleboro was grinding grain into flour. Getting it shipped was a different matter, though, because the railroads were blocked for several days. The round building with the cupola is a storage tank for the city's gas company. (Brattleboro P.H.O.T.O.S.)

*A shoveling crew takes a break after opening a narrow passageway on Mechanic Street in Keene, New Hampshire. (Historical Society of Cheshire County)*

*This Ashuelott Railroad train and its passengers left Keene, New Hampshire's station at 3 p.m. on Monday. Immobilized in the drifts for more than two days, the train retreated to Keene at 5 a.m. on Thursday without ever reaching its destination. (Historical Society of Cheshire County)*

*A banner snow drift at the residence of Deacon Z. K. Graves in West Keene, New Hampshire. (Keene Public Library)*

*Russell and Jack cut a path to the street in front of Russell's Livery Stable in Keene, New Hampshire. (Keene Public Library)*

*Clearing the sidewalks in Manchester, New Hampshire, was an arduous task. A coating of packed ice was found at the bottom of many drifts. (Manchester Historic Association)*

*Wagon and sleigh tracks left deep ruts in the snow along Hanover Street in Manchester, New Hampshire. (Manchester Historic Association)*

# Sources

## Chapter 1:

### The Storm Begins

*New York Times,* March 13, 1888; *Bellows Falls Times,* March 15, 1888.
*Thoughts of the Times: The Connecticut Courant,* March 16, 1888.


## Chapter 2:

### Anatomy of the Blizzard

**Tracing the Storm's Progress:** Everett Hayden, *The Great Storm Off the Atlantic Coast of the United States, March 11th–14th. 1888* (Washington: G.P.O., 1888); Paul J. Kocin, "An analysis of the Blizzard of '88," *Bulletin of the American Meteorological Society* (November 1983); David M. Ludlum, *The Vermont Weather Book* (New Jersey: Rutgers University Press, 1985); United States Signal Service, *Monthly Weather Review* (March 1888); Winslow Upton, "The Storm of March 11–14, '88" *the American Meteorological Journal* (May 1888).
    **How Deep Was It?:** *New Hampshire Union* (Manchester, New Hampshire), March 13, 1888.
    **A New Ice Age?:** *New Hampshire Union,* March 16, 1888.


## Chapter 3:

### The Chronology of The Blizzard

    **The Southern Fringe of the Storm:** *Hartford Times,* March 14, 1888; *Philadelphia Inquirer,* March 13, 1888.
    **New Jersey's Fate:** *Philadelphia Inquirer,* March 13, 14, 1888; *Newark News,* March 12, 1888; *New York Herald,* March 14, 1888. Arthur Grant Balcom, "New Providence-1738–1938," *The Independent Press* (February 7, 1973).
    **New York Confronts the Storm:** *New York Herald,* March 13, 1888; *New York Sun,* March 13, 14, 15, 1888; *Huntington at the Turn of the Century* (Huntington, New York: Huntington Historical Society, 1974); *The Democratic Register* (Ossining, New York), March 17, 1888; *Albany Times,* March 13, 1888.
    **The Blizzard Hits New England:** *Bridgeport Telegram,* March 13, 1888; *The Evening News* (Danbury, Connecticut), March 13, 1888; *New Haven Register,* March 12, 15, 1888; *The American* (Waterbury, Connecticut), March 12, 14, 1888; *The Connecticut Courant,* March 15, 1888; *Hartford Times,* March 14, 1888; *Torrington Register,* March 24, 1888.
    **Massachusetts Bears the Brunt:** *Boston Daily Globe,* March 13, 1888; *West Springfield Record,* April 17, 1975; *Worcester Daily Telegram,* March 13, 1888.
    **Up North:** *New Hampshire Union,* March 12, 14, 1888; *The Phoenix* (Brattleboro, Vermont), March 16, 1888; *Rutland Daily Herald,* March 15, 16, 1888.


## Chapter 4:

### How the Storm Affected People

    Ruth Kirk, *Snow* (New York: William Morrow & Company, 1978); *Cannondale: A Connecticut Neighborhood* (Wilton, Connecticut: Wilton Historical Society, 1987).
    **The Icy Fingers of Death:** William H. Hoy, "Roscoe Conkling Nearly Dead," *New York Sun,* March 14, 1888; Samuel Meredith Strong, *The Great Blizzard of 1888* (publisher unknown, 1938); *New York Sun,* March 15, 1888; *New York Times,* April 19, 1888; *The Evening News,* March 14, 17, 1888; Richard Sevrens, "Legendary Blizzard of '88 Took 400 Lives; Caused $20 Million Damages," *Springfield Daily News,* March 8, 1963; *New York Herald,* March 13, 1888; *Waterbury American,* March 15, 1888; *The Connecticut Courant,* March 15, 1888.

***Beating the Elements—Blizzard Fashions:*** *New York Times,* March 13, 1888; *New York World,* March 13, 1888; *New York Herald,* March 13, 1888; *Concord Evening Monitor* (Concord, New Hampshire), March 13, 1888.

***Hello, Central!:*** *Worcester Daily Telegram,* March 14, 1888; *Hartford Courant,* March 16, 1888.

***The Threat of Fire:*** *Albany Times,* March 13, 1888; *The Sentinel* (Ansonia, Connecticut), March 16, 1888; *New York Sun,* March 14, 1888; *Philadelphia Inquirer,* March 13, 1888.

***Getting Home:*** Recollections of Shamgar Babcock, Elmhurst, New York, as cited in Strong; *The Phoenix,* March 16, 1888.

***The Pub With No Beer:*** *New York Herald,* March 13, 14, 1888.

***The Entrepreneurial Spirit:*** Recollections of Albert Firmin, as cited in Strong; *New York Herald,* March 13, 1888.

***A Cause for Celebration:*** *New Hampshire Union,* March 15, 1888; Julia Pettee, "Lakeville Resident Gives Eye-Witness Tale of Big Snow," from a newspaper clipping in the files of the Falls Village Historical Society, Falls Village, Connecticut (publication and date unknown); *Connecticut Western News* (North Canaan, Connecticut), January 26, 1961.

***Humor in the Snow:*** *White Mountain Republic,* March 16, 1888; Peter Lyon, "The Blizzard of '88," *Holiday* (March 1959); *Newark News,* March 14, 1888; *New York Herald,* March 14, 1888, *New Canaan Messenger,* March 17, 1888; *Hartford Times,* March 14, 1888.

## Chapter 5:

### Stuck! Trying to Get Around in the Blizzard

*New Hampshire Union,* March 13, 1888; *New York Times,* March 14, 1888; *Bridgeport Telegram,* March 13, 1888; *Worcester Daily Telegram,* March 13, 1888.

***The Big City Besieged:*** *New York World,* March 12, 1888; Experiences of Walter Hall as told to L. M. McKibben, as cited in Strong; *New York Herald,* March 13, 1888; Adrian C. Leiby, in collaboration with Albert T. Klyberg, Jr., and Emorie A. Leiby, *The Huguenot Settlement of Schraalenburgh; The History of Bergenfield, New Jersey* (Bergenfield, New Jersey: Bergenfield Free Public Library, 1964); *New York Sun,* March 13, 14, 1888.

***On City Streets:*** *Bridgeport Morning News,* March 13, 1888; *The Evening News,* March 12, 1888; *The Connecticut Courant,* March 16, 1888; *Worcester Daily Telegram,* March 14, 1888; Diary of James F. D. Garfield (Fitchburg Historical Society, Fitchburg, Massachusetts); *New Hampshire Union,* March 12, 1888.

***Fighting the Snow:*** *The Evening News,* March 16, 17, 1888; *The Democratic Register,* March 17, 1888; Leiby; *Newark News,* March 12, 1888; *New York Times,* March 14, 1888; *Peterborough Transcript* (Peterborough, New Hampshire), March 15, 1888.

***Stranded in the Club Car:*** *The Evening News,* March 16, 1888; *New York Herald,* March 14, 1888; *New York World,* March 15, 1888; *The Orange Journal* (Orange, Massachusetts), March 16, 1888; *Westboro Chronotype* (Westboro, Massachusetts), March 17, 1888; *Boston Daily Globe,* March 15, 1888; *Worcester Daily Telegram,* March 13, 1888.

***Disaster at Lewes Harbor:*** *Delaware Gazette and State Journal,* March 22, 1888; *Concord Evening Monitor,* March 17, 1888.

***Havoc on the High Seas:*** *New Haven Evening Register,* March 15, 1888; Letter by Martha K. Hall of Huntington, New York, *Long Island Forum* (September 1944); Lyon; Nat Brandt, "The Great Blizzard of '88," *American Heritage* (February 1977).

## Chapter 6:

### The Business of the Blizzard

***The View From Wall Street:*** *New York Times,* March 13, 14, 1888; *New York Herald,* March 14, 1888; *New York Sun,* March 13, 1888.

***Did You hear the One About the Traveling Salesman?:*** Recollections of A.C. Chadbourne, as cited in Strong.

**A Losing Proposition**: *The Evening News*, March 20, 1888; *Concord Evening Bulletin*, (Concord, New Hampshire), March 13, 1888; *New York Herald*, March 12, 13, 1888; *Electric Age*, March 16, 1888, April 1, 1888.

**Neither Rain, Nor Snow, Nor Gloom of Night?**: *New Hampshire Union*, March 15, 1888; *New York Herald*, March 13, 1888; *New York Times*, March 13, 1888.

## Chapter 7:

### The Aftermath

*Newark News*, March 14, 1888.

**The Threat of Famine**: *New York Sun*, March 15, 1888; *Philadelphia Inquirer*, March 13, 1888; Excerpt from the diary of George Henry Deuell, prepared by George Badgely, *Dutchess County Historical Society Yearbook* (Poughkeepsie, New York: Clinton House Museum, 1984); *Torrington Register*, March 17, 1888; Recollections of Dr. Charles Gilmore, as cited in Strong.

**No Meat Today**: Diary of Anna Maria Nichols, (Trumbull Historical Society, Trumbull, Connecticut); *New York Times*, March 14, 1888; *Boston Daily Globe*, March 15, 1888; Letter by M. Brusselars, as cited in Stong; *New York Sun*, March 15, 1888.

**An Energy Crisis**: *New York Sun*, March 15, 1888; *Philadelphia Inquirer*, March 14, 1888.

**Cleaning Up**: Corydon Bell, *The Wonder of Snow* (New York: Hill and Wang, 1957); *New York Herald*, March 13, 1888; *New York Times*, March 15, 1888; Letter by Henry A. Smith to the Blizzard Men of '88, as cited in Strong; Patrick Hughes, "The Blizzard of 1888," *Weatherwise Magazine* (December 1981); *The Evening News*, March 14, 16, 1888; *Hartford Times*, March 14, 1888; Letter by John J. Meisinger to the Blizzard Men of '88, as cited in Strong; *Concord Evening Monitor*, March 14, 1888; *The Orange Journal*, March 23, 1888; *New Hampshire Sentinel* (Keene, New Hampshire), March 21, 1888.

**Thawing Out**: *The Evening News*, March 16, 1888; Clarence Ashton Wood, "We've Had Our Blizzards," *Long Island Forum* (December 1944); Letter by Margie Crossman, as quoted in *Huntington at the Turn of the Century*.

**The Storm That Changed America**: Stan Fischler, *Uptown, Downtown: A Trip Through Time on New York's Subways* (New York: Hawthorn Books, Inc., 1976); Irving Werstein, *The Blizzard of '88* (New York: Thomas Y. Crowell Company, 1960).

**Preserving the Memories**: J. H. Eddy, "The Great Blizzard of March 1888 and the New Canaan Branch Railroad," *Report of the New Canaan Historical Society*, (New Canaan, Connecticut), 1968; Samuel Meredith Strong, *The Great Blizzard of 1888*, (Publisher unknown, 1938); Program notes to the 1963 meeting of The Blizzard Men and Ladies of 1888 (New York Historical Society).

## Chapter 8:

### Notes On the Storm

**The Other Blizzard of '88**: *New York Times*, January 12–20, 1888.

**Three Centuries of Memorable Snowstorms**: David M. Ludlum, *The American Weather Book* (Houghton Mifflin Company, 1985); David M. Ludlum, *Early American Winters*, (Houghton Mifflin Company, 1966); David M. Ludlum, *The Country Journal New England Weather Book*, (Houghton Mifflin Company, 1976).

## Chapter 9:

### Remembering the Great Storm

Mark Twain Memorial (Hartford, Connecticut).

# Index

*Judd Caplovich, author/researcher,* turned a lifelong interest in things from the past into a full-time occupation in 1980 when he left the computer industry to pursue a career as a dealer in unusual antique mechanical devices, early photography, and ephemera. A native of Worcester, Massachusetts, he currently resides in Vernon, Connecticut.

*Wayne R. Cogan, designer-principal photographer,* is a commercial artist/photographer and an avid collector of pre-1920 antique wooden cameras. He lives and works in West Hartford, Connecticut, and currently serves as president of the Photographic Historical Society of New England.

*Paul J. Kocin, meteorological consultant,* is a research meteorologist specializing in the study of severe weather events at NASA's Goddard Laboratory for Atmospheres in Greenbelt, Maryland. He wrote a technical analysis of the Blizzard of '88 published in the November 1983 issue of the Bulletin of the American Meteorological Society.

*Jim Rigby, chief writer,* is a freelance writer and public relations consultant based in West Hartford, Connecticut. His interest in the Blizzard of '88 was piqued by seeing a collection of 19th century photographs depicting the storm, part of a 1985 exhibition at Hartford's Old State House.

*Wayne W. Westbrook, Ph.D., editor,* teaches creative writing at the University of Connecticut and Communications at Manchester Community College. He resides in Canton, Connecticut.